Teaching and Directing Forensics

Teaching and Directing Forensics

Michael D. Bartanen
Pacific Lutheran University

GSP
Gorsuch Scarisbrick, Publishers
Scottsdale, Arizona

Publisher: John W. Gorsuch
Editor: Nils Anderson
Developmental Editor: Gay L. Pauley
Production Editor: Mary B. Cullen
Sales & Marketing: Don DeLong
Cover Design: Graphics 2
Typesetting: The Job Shop

Gorsuch Scarisbrick, Publishers
8233 Via Paseo del Norte, Suite F-400
Scottsdale, AZ 85258

10 9 8 7 6 5 4 3 2 1

ISBN 0-89787-348-3

Copyright © 1994 by Gorsuch Scarisbrick, Publishers

Printed in the United States of America.

Library of Congress Cataloging-in-Publication Data

Bartanen, Michael D.
    Teaching and directing forensics / Michael D. Bartanen
        p.   cm.
    Includes bibliographical references (p.) and index.
    ISBN 0-89787-348-3
    1. Forensics (Public speaking) — Study and teaching. I. Title.
PN4181.B36 1993
808.5′1′0711 — dc20

93-31147
CIP

Speech Communication Titles from GSP

Communicating in Organizations: A Casebook, Gary L. Peterson, Editor

Communication: Apprehension, Avoidance, and Effectiveness, Third Edition, Virginia P. Richmond and James McCroskey

Communication Between the Sexes: Sex Differences and Sex-Role Stereotypes, Second Edition, Lea P. Stewart et al.

Communication in the Secondary School: A Pedagogy, Third Edition, Ron R. Allen et al.

Conflict: From Theory to Action, Roxane Lulofs

Critical Thinking: The Analysis of Arguments, James A. Herrick

Interpersonal and Relational Communication, Kittie W. Watson and Larry L. Barker

Interviewing: Skills and Applications, James E. Sayer and Lilburn P. Hoehn

Intrapersonal Communication Processes, Charles V. Roberts et al.

Intrapersonal Communication Processes: Original Essays, SPECTRA

Look What Happened to Frog: Storytelling in Education, Pamela J. Cooper and Rives Collins

Managing Communication in Organizations: An Introduction, Second Edition, H. Wayland Cummings et al.

Nonpolicy Debate, Second Edition, Michael D. Bartanen and David A. Frank

Persuasion: Contexts, People, and Messages, Roxane Lulofs

Seeking Compliance: The Production of Interpersonal Influence Messages, James. P. Dillard, Editor

Small Group Discussion: A Theoretical Approach, Second Edition, Charles Pavitt and Ellen Curtis

Speech Communication for the Classroom Teacher, Fourth Edition, Pamela J. Cooper

Teaching and Directing Forensics, Michael D. Bartanen

The Articulate Voice: An Introduction to Voice and Diction, Second Edition, Lynn K. Wells

Understanding Family Communication, Janet Yerby et al.

Contents

PART II: FORENSICS AS TEACHING AND LEARNING   73

7   Judging Forensics Contests   119

8   Learning Resources in Forensics   137

Preface

Forensics has stood the test of time as a valuable educational tool. Each year thousands of college and high school students learn argumentation and speaking skills while participating in forensics events. They compete in activities ranging from highly analytical team debate to highly aesthetic oral interpretation of literature. They experience the joys and frustrations of competition. Forensics programs are found in all 50 states and range from rural high school programs with few participants to urban university programs that may sponsor a hundred or more competitors.

Individuals who teach and coach forensics must be dedicated, "jack-of-all-trade" teachers. They must understand the many kinds of events that make up forensics activity, know how to motivate student competitors, and be able to adapt teaching strategies to the special circumstances of contest speaking. Ironically, no special certification is required for forensics teachers and coaches; indeed, few classes are available from which to learn the necessary skills. Although no single class can cover all contingencies a teacher is likely to encounter given the breadth of program philosophies and activities, many schools do offer a course for new and prospective forensics teachers. This textbook is intended for that course.

Teaching and Directing Forensics helps new and prospective teachers build the teaching skills required for working with a high school or college forensics program. The book provides a strong overview of activities, methods, and goals. It does not attempt to define the "true" or "politically correct" way to teach forensics; instead, it is hoped that each new teacher will explore the many philosophies that guide forensics activity and formulate a philosophy that fits his or her own school, teaching style, and goals. This textbook and the course for which it is designed lay the foundation for teaching success in a challenging field.

The one "truth" of forensics is that it is an integral part of liberal education. Forensics training rewards both students and their teachers. It develops in students the skills necessary for competing in a complex world. It enlightens them, educates them, and often liberates them from prejudice. Forensics offers teachers the opportunity to work with bright, motivated students and help these students begin to achieve their potential.

Acknowledgments

I would like to thank the following individuals, who reviewed this textbook in earlier stages and offered constructive criticism toward its improvement: Greg H. Gardner, Rollins College; Norbert H. Mills, University of Toledo; Colan T. Hanson, North Dakota State University; Eilene Kingsley, McNeese State University; and Lawrence A. Kraft, Eastern Washington University. Thanks also to my wife and colleague, Kristine Bartanen.

1
An Overview of Competitive Speech and Debate

CHAPTER OVERVIEW

This chapter introduces the subject of forensics education. It defines forensics and the usual events that make up competitive forensics. The chapter then presents the educational benefits connected with forensics competition, a brief history of forensics in the United States, and the competing educational philosophies used by teachers and students.

During this school year, thousands of high school and college students will participate in some form of organized speech competition. The kinds of events they will prepare will be as varied as the students themselves. Some events will require intensive preparation, while others will test the speaker's ability to present a coherent speech with only a moment's preparation. Likewise, some events will stress the ability to process information, while others will encourage appreciation of the beauty of a well-written poem. Despite these differences, all these events share a commonality: They provide a unique opportunity for students to learn valuable life skills in an enjoyable, competitive environment.

This text attempts to help the new speech and debate teacher to confront the challenge of helping students prepare for and succeed at competition. The diversity of forensic events may make this task seem daunting. Applying some fundamental communication principles and a healthy dose of common sense can make directing the speech and debate program a rewarding experience.

This chapter defines terms connected with teaching competitive speech and debate, outlines the educational benefits achieved through participating in the activity, provides a brief historical background of the activity in the United States, and previews the rest of the text.

THE DEFINITION OF FORENSICS

Forensics is the term commonly used to describe the myriad of activities connected with competitive speech and debate. In 1974, the first National Developmental Conference on Forensics defined the term:

> Forensics is an educational activity primarily concerned with using an argumentative perspective in examining problems and communicating with people. An argumentative perspective on communication involves the study of reason given by people as justification for acts, beliefs, attitudes, and values. From this perspective, forensics activities, including debate and individual events, are laboratories for helping students to understand and communicate various forms of argument more effectively in a variety of contexts with a variety of audiences.[1]

The conference participants deliberately chose to call forensics a "laboratory." Students, in the forensic laboratory, "experiment" with various communicative strategies to improve their abilities at persuasion. This experimentation normally happens in a competitive framework known as the forensic tournament. The tournament format allows students to compete against others to win awards, usually in the form of trophies or certificates. Forensics is thus a form of experiential learning designed to improve skills in reasoning, public communication, and aesthetic appreciation.

Forensic activities are divided into three main categories: debate, public address, and oral interpretation. There are many different events included in each of these categories. Figure 1.1 lists some of the common events but it does not show the wide variety in the number of traditional and nontraditional events, the rules, or the competitive practices. Rapid growth in individual events over the past 20 years (such as public address and oral interpretation events) has led to increasing use of nontraditional events in college and high school tournaments. It should also be stressed that rules guiding these events are not uniform. A unique characteristic of competitive forensics is the democratic nature of the activity: Individual tournaments adapt rules and events either whimsically or in response to an experimental urge.

Debate events are the oldest and most traditional of the three forensic events. Regardless of a particular format, all debates share several characteristics: two sides, a debatable resolution, equal time limits, and both structural and situational constraints guiding the participants.[2] *Public address events* train students in public speaking by giving them experience in adapting to different speech purposes, such as informing, persuading, or entertaining. These events are most similar to the speaking taking place in classroom speech courses. *Oral interpretation events* are the most recent addition to competitive forensics. These events train students in the performance and appreciation of the literary genres. While originally designed

FIGURE 1.1 Commonly used forensic events.

DEBATE:	Cross-examination team debate
	Oxford team debate
	Lincoln-Douglas debate
	Parliamentary debate
	Student congress
	Discussion
PUBLIC ADDRESS:	Persuasive speaking (oratory)
	Informative speaking (expository)
	Extemporaneous speaking
	Impromptu speaking
	Communication analysis
	After dinner speaking
	Rhetorical criticism
	Argument analysis
	Radio speaking (editorial commentary)
ORAL INTERPRETATION:	Programmed reading
	Poetry
	Prose
	Dramatic interpretation
	Humorous interpretation
	Duo interpretation
	Reader's theater

to be distinct from acting, by requiring use of manuscripts and multiple selections, much of the distinction has disappeared over time. Contemporary theory emphasizes the performance elements of oral interpretation over the analytical elements. Current practice gives contestants more flexibility in choosing materials for contest events than was true in earlier years. Contemporary contests often do not require participants to maintain the illusion of reading a manuscript. This blurs the distinction between performance on the theater stage and the performance in a classroom.

Educators introduced these diverse activities into their curriculum to accomplish many goals, and while every event accomplishes educational objectives in different ways, their commonality is the belief that forensics competition is an effective educational tool.

THE EDUCATIONAL BENEFITS OF FORENSICS

How do students benefit from forensics competition? As with other elements of a liberal education, it is difficult to be quantitatively precise about the effects of forensic training on individual students. For many years, it seemed sufficient to use anecdotal evidence to justify the activity. Leading political figures, business tycoons, and educators supplied their personal testimony about the importance of their own forensic training on their careers.[3] Shrinking resources for education have made justification of all co-curricular activities a higher priority. While there is no definitive justification for forensics, there are several important essays and studies providing evidence about the unique benefit of forensic training.[4] For example, the late professor of debate Daniel Rohrer described debate as a part of a liberal arts education.[5] His justifications of debate—for improving critical thinking and decision-making processes— apply equally well to other forms of competition. In general, forensics provides students with four primary benefits.

First, *forensic training is valuable career preparation.* Forensic training is asserted to be an important means of preparing for careers in law, politics, and other public professions.[6] Indeed, law and politics are fields traditionally associated with debate training, and many members of Congress and other career politicians cite debate training as important to their success. These findings are primarily anecdotal (asking prominent people about their evaluation of their forensic training) or surveys of admissions counselors, law school deans, and other career decision-makers.[7]

Second, *forensic training is a valuable educational supplement.* Several studies suggest that training in debate and public speaking provides students with greater proficiency at public communication. Forensics training also is cited as an important way for students to overcome mild or moderate communication anxiety, to develop study skills and time allocation skills,[8] and for learning critical thinking and reasoning.[9]

Third, *forensics gives students valuable insights into public policy and civic concerns.* The content of most forensic events are issues of public interest or policies under consideration by policy-makers. Educators usually frame debate topics to encourage students to consider key policy and to value the implications of issues confronting society. Choosing issues that have two sides creates the necessity for students to acquaint themselves with various perspectives while gathering the evidence and analysis they will need in the debate round.

Students participating in public address and oral interpretation events follow a similar pattern. They often choose topics they expect audiences will be interested in or concerned about. There is usually no percentage in choosing a trivial topic for a persuasive or informative speech since audiences usually consider the significance of the topic in judging the effectiveness of the speech and speaker.[10] While oral interpreters have greater latitude in selecting materials for their aesthetic value, they often choose literature that addresses either contemporary concerns or universal themes with contemporary applications.

The fourth benefit of forensics training is that *it builds courage and a sense of personal growth and satisfaction.* Students participate in part because they believe they will become more capable people who will be able to handle themselves in a wider range of contexts. Effective public speaking requires courage and the ability to adapt successfully to audiences. Mastering the rudiments of public speaking expands the repertoire of situations that students feel prepared to handle.

In summary, forensics is educationally valuable for career preparation, as an educational supplement, as a way to learn more about current issues, and as a way to build courage and a greater sense of personal growth. While not the only means of securing these benefits, the enjoyable and competitive nature of forensics encourages the achievement of them. Knowledge of this relation helps to explain the historical popularity of forensics activities.

A BRIEF HISTORY OF FORENSICS IN THE UNITED STATES

While the teaching and learning of public speaking and debate are very old, competition in those activities is relatively new. The teaching of debate dates as far back as the Classical period in ancient Greece. Greek civilization saw important benefits in citizens mastering effective communication skills. Thus, the Greeks were responsible for nurturing the emergence of rhetoric.

Rhetoric professors Lester Thonssen and A. Craig Baird called Greek philosopher Protagoras (481–411 B.C.) the "father of debate."[11] Protagoras created themes on which his students developed and presented arguments for and against. He apparently recognized the importance of students understanding both sides of an issue in preparing to be active citizens.

Aristotle's work *The Rhetoric* is the most influential contribution to Western understanding of the role of public speaking in human affairs. Aristotle crafted a system of rhetoric, grouped around themes like the nature of proofs, which remains essential to contemporary rhetorical theory.[12] Roman and medieval theorists elaborated on Aristotelian themes and began to develop learning strategies. They introduced strategies such as rigorous training and preparation in disputes, the study of great speakers, and the presentation and criticism of ideas and theories that would eventually become the foundation for forensics education in the twentieth century.

Immigrants to the New World brought their interest in speech and debate. Citizens created literary societies to discuss and debate important ideas. These debates were very lax in structure. On the other hand, university students engaged in "disputations" that were highly structured discussions of logical questions, often conducted in Latin. These disputations later evolved into more flexible formats that became very popular in the nineteenth century.[13] Schools and literary societies began discussing debate questions using teams whose numbers ranged from 2 to 20. There was also wide variation in the number of speeches that each team gave on their side of the question as well as variety in the role of the audiences in the debates.

Eventually college debate societies began publicly to debate each other. These contests were very popular and attracted crowds.[14] The debates often took an entire day and were accompanied by considerable ritual and fanfare, not unlike contemporary sports contests. While their structure differed from contemporary debates, the contests rapidly generated interest in debate. By the turn of the century many colleges and, later, high schools formed clubs to debate other schools.[15]

The formation of clubs increased organization of the activity and standardized the process. Schools began to hire teachers to "coach" students in debate. In early contests, the participating schools negotiated the contest rules and topics. This was undoubtedly very time consuming and led to creation of leagues and honor societies whose functions included standardizing rules and procedures and encouraging student interest.[16] This rapidly led to giving students academic credit for their debate work, and books and articles about debate theory began to appear. It would, however, take many years to completely standardize debate practice.

The development of high school activities followed a similar progression. Many schools taught declamation (recitation) and other speaking and debate activities as early as 1825.[17] Gradually, leagues were formed and contests were held in debate and in declamation, oration, discussion, and oral interpretation.[18] The first national high school forensics organization, the National Forensic League (NFL), was created in 1925. The NFL sponsored regional and national contests and other recognitions for speakers, teachers, and programs. There are other high school organizations, such as the National Catholic Forensic League, but the NFL has always been the largest high school forensics organization.

The 1920s saw forensic activities blossom. An emerging highway and road system expanded travel opportunities, and the tournament format began with an event at Southwestern College in 1923.[19] National debate topics were selected for use, and individual events continued to blossom in popularity.

Forensics grew rapidly until the 1960s. The National Debate Tournament (NDT) began in 1947 as a national championship for college policy debate. Forensics educators formed the American Forensic Association

(AFA) as a national professional organization. International debate activity was popular and there was some experimentation with television debate in the early 1960s. Unfavorable economic conditions in the early 1970s lessened the number of forensics programs, but eventually the activity stabilized in the amount of programs. National championship tournaments in individual events and nonpolicy debate also were introduced for college participants.[20]

Economic conditions and lingering questions about the precise educational benefits of forensics continue to challenge the activity. Recent economic downturns have severely pinched higher education. The resulting resource scarcity has led to the cutback or cancellation of many programs, particularly at state supported institutions. One side effect is fewer college programs training qualified high school teachers. This has created a shortage of qualified coaches and has led to situations where individuals without forensics training are drafted to direct high school programs. There are no national statistics on the number of qualified teachers available because few states have established guidelines for certifying forensics teachers.[21]

This puts additional pressure on high school programs. Many states do not recognize speech communication as a high school competency area. Increasingly fewer high school teachers are extensively trained in speech communication education. They often are forced to double as theater or journalism teachers. Or they may feel comfortable teaching public speaking but unqualified to teach debate. This does not bode well for the long-term health of the activity at either the high school or college level.

Occasionally, high schools and colleges attempt to sponsor student-run programs. These programs operate with minimal or nonexistent faculty sponsorship and are inevitably weaker than programs with strong faculty leadership. The students rarely have training in teaching methods; they may not have a philosophy of competition that is healthy or productive, and they may not even know how to manage the complex logistics of participating in a tournament. This will inevitably lead to frustration for the participants and the quick disappearance of the program.

Forensics has changed considerably since its emergence in the nineteenth century. Different formats, events, and theories have all combined to make competitive speech far different from the public contests of the 1880s. In good times and bad, however, forensics has remained a valuable part of a liberal arts education.

THE PHILOSOPHY OF THIS TEXT

This text will attempt to present a wide view of the philosophy of forensics. You will quickly see that there is no one theory or philosophy of the activity that dominates writing and thinking. At the same time, it is important to justify the philosophy of this text. It will help you to evaluate subsequent discussions and hopefully encourage you to clarify your own philosophy about forensics. Reasonable people differ about their approach to the activity and its underlying philosophies. There is increasing healthy discussion about the comparative value of different philosophical approaches.

There are at least three general philosophical approaches that participants adopt toward forensics education. These include: forensics as *rhetorical training,* forensics as an *intellectual game,* and forensics as a *competitive activity.* Before briefly distinguishing between these perspectives we must warn you that they are not completely distinct. They share some common assumptions about theory and practice. They also should be viewed as general guides to how educators view the activity, *not* as distinct "union cards."

This book will emphasize forensics as a method of *rhetorical training.* This view grounds forensic training in the rhetorical traditions that inspired its original development. The rhetorical perspective considers forensics to be a form of communication where communicators develop good reasons to help audiences make rational decisions. This requires communicators to be both audience-centered and adaptive to a wide range of listeners.

The rhetorical approach is the traditional perspective of argumentation and public speaking textbooks. Forensics as an *intellectual game,* however, is more recent as a philosophical approach. This philosophy conceives of forensics as a means of emphasizing the critical thinking and problem solving abilities of individual students. This emphasis allows students to take a wide latitude in creating arguments and strategies in game playing,[22] and places less emphasis on the public communication elements of forensics and, to an extent, deemphasizes the need for audience adaptation.

The third approach, forensics as a *competitive activity,* considers forensics merely as a form of competition. This perspective considers the activity from a rule-bound view. It emphasizes creating a "level playing field" of competition for the participants. Decisions about event rules, tournament management, and other competition issues are emphasized. Philosophical issues take a lower precedence.

Each of these philosophies is useful in understanding forensics. Each of these approaches is both strong and weak when used to make educational decisions. The rhetorical perspective, for example, is strongest in its emphasis on the audience-related variables of competition. It is weaker in terms of occasionally discouraging the use of innovative arguments and theories. The games perspective would be just the opposite, stronger in innovation, weaker in encouraging adaptation. The activity perspective is useful in encouraging standardization of practices, such as individual events competition rules, but weaker in providing a clear educational rationale for competitive choices.

There are elements of both the games and activities perspectives throughout the text. The major emphasis, however, is on attempting to understand forensics from a rhetorical perspective. In addition, it attempts to use other communication theory ideas in our discussion, applies ideas from organizational and interpersonal theories, and also applies a good deal of common sense. Common sense is, by far, the best rule for learning and teaching forensics.

PLAN FOR THE TEXT

The text is divided into two major parts: The first part describes forensics as an activity; the second part analyzes teaching and learning strategies and examines ethical and philosophical issues. The first part attempts to describe "what" forensics is. The second part introduces "how" it is learned, and considers its "ideal practices" and some learning resources.

Chapters 2, 3, and 4 survey the forensic activity from the general systems theory perspective, identifying the three major systems making up the activity. These systems include forensics as organizational systems, forensics as an educational and competitive system, and forensics as an interpersonal system.

The second part develops teaching and learning strategies for forensics. Chapters 5, 6, 7, and 8 discuss teaching strategies for debate, individual events, judging, and available learning resources. The final chapter introduces philosophical and ethical issues in forensics education.

This text is not intended as a complete step-by-step guide to teaching forensics. You soon will see that there is no single method of learning and teaching forensics. Forensics education sometimes seems to be a "blooming and buzzing confusion" of activities and teaching techniques. The goal of this text is to help you sort through this, to organize this apparent confusion, and discover and formulate useful learning philosophies and teaching techniques that fit your own teaching methods and the unique characteristics of your school and students.

ACTIVITIES

1. If your school or college has a forensics program, survey some of the student participants. What have they learned through their participation? How do they see forensics as different from their other classes?

2.   Discuss the three philosophies of forensics introduced at the end of this chapter. Which one fits your own educational philosophy? What are the strengths and weaknesses of these philosophies?

3.   Measurement of educational outcomes is becoming a very important issue in both secondary and post-secondary education. How might educators assess the educational benefits of forensics participation? Are there measures besides anecdotal reports that might clarify the value of forensics?

NOTES

1. James H. McBath, ed., *Forensics as Communication: The Argumentative Perspective.* (Skokie: National Textbook, 1975), p. 11.

2. Michael D. Bartanen and David A. Frank, *Debating Values.* (Scottsdale: Gorsuch Scarisbrick, 1990).

3. R. C. Huseman and D. M. Goodman, "Editor's Corner: BYD Congressional Questionnaire." *Journal of the American Forensic Association,* 12 (1976): 226.

4. Kent Colbert and Thompson Biggers, "Why Should We Support Debate?" *Journal of the American Forensic Association,* 21 (1985): 237–240. Bill Hill, "Intercollegiate Debate: Why Do Students Bother?" *Southern Speech Communication Journal,* 48 (1982): 77–88. Stephen C. Wood and Pamela A. Rowland-Morin, "Motivational Tension: Winning vs. Pedagogy in Academic Debate." *National Forensic Journal,* 7 (1989): 81–98.

5. Daniel M. Rohrer, "Debate as a Liberal Art." In David A. Thomas and Jack Hart, eds., *Advanced Debate,* 3rd ed. (Larchwood: National Textbook, 1987).

6. James H. McBath, "Speech and the Legal Profession." *Speech Teacher,* 10 (1961): 44–47. A. Pollock, "The Relationship of a Background in Scholastic Forensics to Effective Communication in the Legislative Assembly." *Speaker and Gavel,* 19 (1982): 17. These are two of many articles discussing the application of forensics to various professions.

7. Robert S. Littlefield, "An Assessment of University Administrators: Do They Value Competitive Debate and Individual Events Programs?" *National Forensic Journal,* 9 (1991): 87–96.

8. I. F. Rothenberg and J. Berman, "College Debate and Effective Writing." *Teaching Political Science,* 8 (1980): 21–39.

9. H. L. Ruff, "Teaching Philosophy and Debate." *Speaker and Gavel,* 17 (1980): 162–170.

10. As will be discussed in the chapter on individual events.

11. Lester Thonssen and A. Craig Baird, *Speech Criticism.* (New York: Ronald Press, 1948).

12. Aristotle, *The Rhetoric.* In R. Robert, trans., *The Works of Aristotle.* (Oxford: Clarendon Press, 1924).

13. G. V. Bohman, "Rhetorical Practice in Colonial America." In Karl W. Wallace, *History of Speech Education in America.* (New York: Appleton-Century-Crofts, 1954). Donald F. Faules, Richard D. Rieke, and Jack Rhodes, *Directing*

Forensics: Contest and Debate Speaking, 2nd ed. (Denver: Morton Publishing, 1976).

14. E. R. Nichols, "A Historical Sketch of Intercollegiate Debating." *Quarterly Journal of Speech*, XXII (1936): 213.

15. L. L. Cowperthwaite and A. C. Baird, "Intercollegiate Debating." In Wallace, *Speech Education in America*.

16. Honor societies included Delta Sigma Rho (organized in 1906), Tau Kappa Alpha (1908), Pi Kappa Delta (1913), and Phi Rho Pi (1928). These are all college organizations. Delta Sigma Rho and Tau Kappa Alpha later merged. Phi Rho Pi is a community college organization.

17. G. L. Borchers and L. R. Wagner, "Speech Education in Nineteenth-Century Schools." In Wallace, *Speech Education in America*.

18. Paul A. Carmack, "The Development of State High School Speech Leagues." *The Speech Teacher*, III (1954): 264–268. Edward D. Shurter, "State Organization for Contests in Public Speaking." *Quarterly Journal of Speech*, I (1915): 59–64.

19. Nichols, "A Historical Sketch of Intercollegiate Debating."

20. The National Forensic Association has hosted a National Individual Events Championship since 1971. The American Forensic Association introduced a second National Individual Events tournament in 1981. The Cross-Examination Debate Association (CEDA) first hosted a national college debate championship in 1986.

21. Several states, such as Wisconsin and Illinois, have moved toward certification of forensics teachers and contest judges. Information about these programs can be obtained from the National Forensic League or the National Association of State High School Activity Associations.

22. Cf. A. C. Snyder, "Ethics in Academic Debate: A Gaming Perspective." In David A. Thomas and Jack Hart, eds., *Advanced Debate*, 4th ed. (Larchwood National Textbook), 1987, pp. 15–29.

Part I
FORENSICS FROM A SYSTEMS PERSPECTIVE

Chapter 2
Forensics as an Organizational System

Chapter 3
Forensics as an Educational System: The Tournament

Chapter 4
Forensics as an Interpersonal and Organizational System: The Program

This first part of the text describes the current nature of forensics activity. Chapter 2 examines the nature and organization of the activity on a national level. Chapter 3 introduces the forensic tournament as the principal teaching and learning arena, and Chapter 4 looks at the forensic program as the basis of forensics education. At the end of Part I you should understand something of the complex nature of forensics as an activity and as a form of experiential learning.

2
Forensics as
an Organizational System

CHAPTER OVERVIEW

This chapter describes how forensics is organized as a collection of systems. It describes the structure of both high school and college forensics, and the important national, state, and local organizational elements of each activity. The chapter then discusses the strengths and weaknesses of organizational structure and some of the ways in which high school and college forensics interact.

SYSTEMS THEORY

In this and the next two chapters, we will use *systems theory* to examine the activity, the tournament, and the program. You might be familiar with systems theory — it is a common tool in communication and other disciplines,[1] and there are many articles and books studying communication from a systems perspective. The reason systems theory is commonly applied in communication research is its utility in describing organisms and their relation to other organisms and the environment. Figure 2.1 lists the various forensics systems, arranged according to their complexity.

Systems theory has many characteristics. Several of these characteristics are particularly important in understanding the various forensics systems diagrammed in Figure 2.1.

FIGURE 2.1 Forensics systems.

15

1. *Systems are collections of subsystems and suprasystems.* Systems follow the nesting principle. Any system consists of smaller systems and is a part of a larger one. When we discuss the forensic activity later in this chapter, we must think about it as a collection of forensics programs at individual high schools and colleges. These programs are, in turn, made up of people participating in forensics tournaments. These tournaments consist of individual competitive rounds. Thus, factors influencing the activity in a general sense will ultimately affect individual competitive rounds, and vice versa.

2. *Systems interact with their environment.* Forensics is one subsystem of a larger educational system. Financial pressures and changes in general educational practice and philosophy influence the nature and conduct of the forensics activity. In recent years, for example, financial problems in state and local educational systems have challenged the abilities of schools to maintain active forensics programs.

3. *Systems strive for balance.* Systems tend toward activities that maintain a balanced state among their components. Forensics, as a system, is characterized by many rules and processes designed to maintain balance in competitive equality. Forensics educators spend much time refining rules and processes to maintain that balance. Standardization of individual events rules, ethical codes, and eligibility rules for participating in particular competitive divisions are all examples of attempting to create and maintain balance in forensics systems.

4. *Systems evolve.* Systems do not remain static but inevitably change and adapt. This evolution can be positive or negative. Positive evolution happens when systems recognize and correct shortcomings. Negative evolution happens when systems evolve into closed systems where they resist change. Systemic evolution is an important characteristic of contemporary forensics. As you will see, practice for debate and individual events has evolved in recent years, and the organization of forensics also is considerably different from its form even 20 years ago. At the same time, there remains much concern about negative entropy in forensics. Some fear that forensics is not adapting to challenges created by concerns regarding educational practices, such as fast delivery in debate.[2]

With these systemic characteristics in mind, we now consider forensics as an organizational system. As a complex organization, forensics is organized into national, regional, state, and local organizations. Each of these organizations has different goals and procedures, some of which work at cross purposes with other organizations. In its most general sense, forensics itself is a subsystem of the larger educational system.

Competitive forensics is a form of experiential learning. While experiential learning is popular in contemporary educational theory, experiential learning as a learning strategy is hardly new. Both Greek and Roman rhetoricians used hypothetical situations and practice to teach students communication and analysis skills. They were the first teachers to use games and simulations to help students learn skills and theories. Game playing is commonly used to teach a wide range of behaviors and skills: Children use rhymes to learn the alphabet, physical games to learn athletic skills and rules of fair play, and simulations to understand everything from war to social interaction skills.

As noted in Chapter 1, teachers in the latter half of the nineteenth and beginning of the twentieth centuries developed the structure of forensics by modeling the activity as an educational simulation. Forensics rapidly developed beyond the schoolroom into a national activity for both high school and college students. By the 1930s, both high school and college forensics had a national organizational structure. Educators made efforts to standardize events and rules and to run national championships. Today, forensics has a distinct and significant national organizational structure. The end of this chapter examines this structure to provide a panorama of the activity and to create a context for the continuing chapter discussions.

And while there is much overlap between high school and college forensics, they are two different systems. There is some interface between the two but generally they function separately. The following discussions briefly sketch the individual systems of high school and college forensics.

THE STRUCTURE OF HIGH SCHOOL FORENSICS

High school forensics consists of a supra-system and 50 individual state systems. Each state is further divided into various leagues and organizations. For example, an individual state might have two or more districts organized along the same lines as organized sports leagues. Private high schools might also belong to other organizations, such as the National Catholic Forensic League. These individual systems are unique and responsive to the idiosyncrasies of their location. Washington state forensics, for example, responds to different influences than does South Carolina. Some differences are geographically inspired, others are due to discrepancies in state educational systems.

Travel patterns in the West are different because of the longer distances between tournaments. Some states have tighter regulations of activities than do others. Washington state, for example, limits the number of class days a student can miss when participating in forensics, while California does not have such a regulation.

The national system of high school forensics consists mainly of two elements—debate topic selection and the National Forensic League (NFL).

Debate Topic Selection

The high school policy debate topic is chosen through a complicated process. A national topic selection committee selects topic areas (for example, poverty) and frames alternative wordings for each topic area. State organizations then vote on topic areas and select a topic wording within the area for use during the debate season. While most states select the same topic wording, occasionally there are different ones selected by individual states.

The National Forensic League selects Lincoln-Douglas debate topics and announces them in its publication, *The Rostrum*. The topics are changed regularly, often every other month, so that students will prepare on several topics during the debate season. The topics are typically "value" resolutions as opposed to the "policy" resolutions used in team debate. Some individual tournaments and states sometimes use their own Lincoln-Douglas topics rather than the ones selected by the NFL.

National Forensic League

The National Forensic League (NFL) is the national fraternal organization of many high school programs that participate in high school forensics.[3] The NFL was founded in 1925 and serves several functions: it gives awards for participation and success in forensics contests, publishes a magazine, and sponsors a national championship tournament.

The NFL bases its system of awards on a point system, allotting points for participating in contests and additional points for being successful at tournament contests. The NFL system arranges these points in a pyramid in which earning more points creates additional degrees of membership. The degrees of membership include: merit (25 points), honor (75 points), excellence (150 points), distinction (250 points), special distinction (750 points), and outstanding distinction (1000 points).

The monthly magazine, *The Rostrum*, publishes articles about the fraternity and forensics practice during the school year. The national tournament is held in June and is the largest high school tournament in the nation. Contestants qualify for the tournament through success at qualifying tournaments held in each NFL district.

The NFL consists of a national organization, district organizations, and local chapters. The local chapter, the basic unit, exists in high schools meeting membership criteria. Chapters are organized into districts of which size and composition are determined by the national organization. The function of the district organization is hosting the district qualifier tournament.

An important characteristic of both the topic selection process and the NFL are their nonbinding nature. States are free to select their own debate topic, and schools need not belong to the NFL. While most states use the same topic, it is not unusual for them to use alternate topics. This is even more true regarding individual events rules and Lincoln-Douglas debate topics. While the NFL provides event guidelines and announces its topics, those guidelines and topics are not always followed.

Each state has its own organizational structure for forensics. This often takes the form of a state organization associated with the agency responsible for athletics and other activities, such as music. These state organizations do many things. They usually supply information about tournaments, provide liability insurance for attending events, and often create eligibility rules and standards for participation. They also may host state tournament finals. Some states, such as Texas, also have curricular guidelines for the forensics class if it is taught at the high school.

Most states are divided into districts for the purposes of competition. Each district usually will have tournaments and a certain number of slots allocated to them for competition at the state tournament. Often the districts will be governed by a committee of educators responsible for administering events and making policies.

Finally, each high school program is a part of a school system with individual characteristics. The school and its system may have strict policies on student participation in activities. In turn, school systems vary widely on compensating teachers of activities and teams, as well as on funding levels for activities and teams. Unfortunately, wide variation in funding levels of both public and private school systems is still a national reality, creating wide differences in the size and competitiveness of high school programs.

THE STRUCTURE OF COLLEGE FORENSICS

College forensics is a bit less complex as a system than is high school. In the first place, it encompasses fewer active programs. There are fewer than a thousand college programs active in various forensic organizations, although there may be more programs that compete only in on-campus events. Second, there are fewer legal and administrative restrictions on college programs. High school programs are subject to a wide range of legal and administrative guidelines from states and localities. Colleges, since the decline in use of the *in loco parentis* philosophy, do not have as many responsibilities for student supervision or as many restrictions on the number or kinds of tournaments that the school can attend.

College forensics is divided into national, regional, and local systems. The most important of these systems are national and local. This differs from high school forensics, where the regional (state) system tends to dominate the activity. National organizations have a strong influence on the nature of college forensics. Figure 2.2 diagrams the national level organization of college forensics.

National Organizations

You may observe considerable fragmentation in the national organization of college forensics. Each of these national organizations and fraternities has different functions and philosophies. Sometimes they work together, other times they work at cross-purposes.

The American Forensic Association (AFA) is a national organization first founded by people attempting to strengthen and promote competitive forensics.[4] In more recent times, the AFA has broadened its interests to include the study of argumentation theory. The AFA sponsors the National Debate Tournament (NDT) and the National Individual Events Tournament (NIET).

The NDT is the oldest national championship tournament for college debate, governed by a national committee and a set of by-laws. The NDT has traditionally debated policy propositions written by a national topic committee and voted on by educators who are members of the AFA, NDT, or one of the fraternities. The NDT is divided nationally into districts. The

FIGURE 2.2   College forensics at the national level. National organizations, their sponsored tournaments, and their affiliated publications.

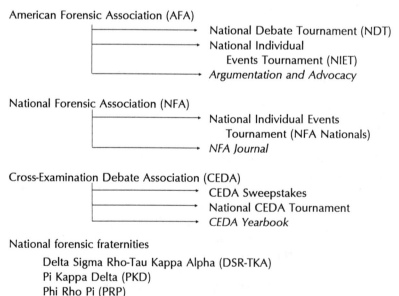

NDT allocates each district a certain number of slots at the tournament, based on the number of school members and their success at the tournament. Each district then holds a district qualifier to select its representatives. Additional participants qualify through at-large qualification systems.

The NIET is organizationally similar. Competitors qualify for the tournament through qualification procedures determined by the NIET committee and the districts. In the NIET students qualify at-large by placing at tournaments according to a formula. In addition, each district holds a tournament for qualification.

Both the NDT and NIET charge school membership dues that help to finance their activities. These tournaments are also underwritten by the AFA. Membership in these groups is open to any school wishing to pay the dues, and schools may participate in the NDT and NIET without being members of the AFA.

The AFA also publishes the journal *Argumentation and Advocacy,* which includes articles about forensics and argumentation theory. The AFA also sponsors professional programs at the national Speech Communication Association (SCA) convention. The SCA is a national professional organization for people interested in communication. Membership is open to both college and high school educators.[5] Most college forensics organizations hold business meetings and sponsor programs at SCA conventions.

The National Forensic Association (NFA) sponsors the oldest of the two Individual Events national tournaments.[6] The NFA also publishes a professional journal, the *National Forensic Journal,* which publishes articles on a wide range of forensics-related subjects.

The Cross-Examination Debate Association (CEDA) was created in 1971 as an alternative to NDT debate.[7] The organization debates two topics a year (as opposed to the single-year topic of the NDT) and usually debates value propositions. The organization publishes a monthly sweepstakes standings report and awards regional and national sweepstakes. CEDA also hosts a national championship tournament and publishes an annual journal, *The CEDA Yearbook,* which publishes articles primarily in value debate theory.

In addition, there are also three forensic honor societies. As noted in Chapter 1, these honor societies were originally created to stimulate interest in forensics among college students. Delta Sigma Rho-Tau Kappa Alpha and Pi Kappa Delta are fraternities for four-year colleges; Phi Rho Pi is for two-year colleges.[8] Each honor society has its own national and regional organizational structure. Individual students join the honor societies by meeting certain membership qualifications. The fraternities each host a national tournament and sponsor convention programs at the SCA national convention. Each fraternity sponsors competition in both CEDA and NDT debate, and the various individual events.

Schools may (1) belong to and participate in the activities of more than one national organization and (2) belong to one fraternity. Most college programs belong to at least one organization but not necessarily to a fraternity. These organizations usually conduct their business through national membership meetings held at their national tournament or with the national SCA convention.

Regional Organizations

College forensics has some regional organizations, but the use of regions tends to be for specific purposes, such as sweepstakes awards or qualification for national tournaments. College programs often compete at tournaments without regard to region, and the regional boundaries used by the various organizations do not always reflect the travel patterns of the programs contained in the region. Many programs perceive the national championships sponsored by the various organizations as more important than regional championships. There are, however, many college programs that are exclusively regional in the nature of their travel, so many opportunities remain open to them. There are more than three hundred college forensics tournaments held each year.[9]

Community colleges are the only programs to make widespread use of state systems. There are state championships for community colleges in several states. This is a major difference between high school and college programs.

The most important systemic component of college forensics is the local program. College programs vary widely in their organization and philosophy, and are usually not affected by the strong administrative framework of high school programs. Most high school programs are closely regulated by legal and administrative rules, since schools have more responsibility for individual students and have existing competitive frameworks for sports competition and other activities. There is no parallel structure at the college level. Each individual college determines the nature of its program, its administration, and its funding.

College programs often are housed within speech communication departments, although that is not always true. Some programs are exclusively administration-supported, or are sponsored within student activity structures, or even housed within other academic departments. Most programs that can be identified as successful, however, have strong ties to the speech communication discipline.[10]

Programs are managed either by faculty sponsors, directed by graduate students, or operated as student-run clubs. The preferable route is through faculty sponsorship. The faculty person (often called the Director of Forensics or the forensics coach) is responsible for both the administration and teaching functions. The person is sometimes given release time or other compensation. Usually, the college or university expects the Director of Forensics to perform the other teaching, research, and service activities normally expected of a faculty member. This can make the forensics position a difficult responsibility and causes considerable turnover in the position.

Many programs provide the forensics director with assistants such as graduate students to help with forensic activities. Unlike college sports, however, this assistance is not as usual nor as well defined. The differences between forensics and sports also extends to funding. Funding may come from administrative or departmental funds, student fees, or donations. Forensic programs are not as well funded as major athletic programs. Being less publicly visible and less clearly associated with the image of the university, forensic programs are less successful in attracting university and off-campus dollars.

The final organizational characteristic of college programs is their usual status as a co-curricular activity. Participants vary in their levels of interest and involvement. Some students use forensics as their major co-curricular activity, while others are more casual users. Students may participate in forensics voluntarily. Many don't receive significant financial aid or academic credit for participation. They also may have rigorous class schedules and part-time jobs competing for their time and attention.

THE INTERFACE BETWEEN COLLEGE AND HIGH SCHOOL FORENSICS

The two previous sections demonstrate the considerable systemic differences between high school and college programs. There are, however, some areas where the two activities overlap. These areas are important to understanding the general scope and nature of the activity.

1. *Both high school and college forensics use similar theories and practices.* A person listening to a round of competition would not, for the most part, find great differences between forensics at either level. Each has some unique events, of course, and important regional differences. But the theories and skills used will be similar. Innovations in debate theory, for example, often begin at the college level and gradually diffuse to high school debate. Many high school forensics teachers, in fact, participate in college programs. Conversely, even more of the judges at high school tournaments are or were college students. These same students often help teach high school programs or summer workshops.

The "trickle-down" of theory and practice from the college to high school level is a point of contention for some high school educators. There is concern that high school students are adopting skills and behaviors (such as rapid delivery in debate) inconsistent with educational goals. This leads to an occasional sense of uneasiness about the relationship of college and high school programs.

2. *High school tournaments are an important source of funding and recruitment for college programs.* Many active college programs regularly host high school tournaments on their campuses. These tournaments, besides providing a service to the community, are also an important method of raising travel funds and attracting potential students to the college.[11] Even if students do not participate in the college program, they may be attracted to the campus or its programs by being on the campus itself. One justification for college forensics is its value in attracting students.

The implication here is that high school and college programs are more interconnected than might be intuitively obvious. High school programs depend on college programs to provide judges for tournaments, new teachers for programs, and innovations in theory and practice. College programs depend on high school programs to provide new participants, revenue, and justification by being a method of recruitment. While there is inevitably uneasiness when two diverse systems coexist, the commonalities outweigh the differences in understanding both activities.

THE EDUCATIONAL IMPLICATIONS OF THE ORGANIZATIONAL STRUCTURES OF FORENSICS

A system's organizational structure influences its function and behavior. In college athletics, for example, the National Collegiate Athletic Association (NCAA) is a powerful force in determining how athletics are perceived and conducted at all levels. NCAA regulations on grade-point averages for incoming students, for example, affect not only recruitment of potential athletes but standards in high school education as well. Similarly, the organizational structure of American forensics influences its practice in several ways.

1. *American forensics lacks a strong national framework for practice.*

Neither high school nor college forensics functions organizationally from the "top down." While programs look nationally for some guidance (most notably in selection of debate topics and to host national championships) they depend more on local and regional support systems.

The national organizations are mostly bureaucratic rather than visionary. Rather than guiding practices they fill particular needs, such as awarding points (NFL), hosting a national tournament (NDT and NIET), or distributing a sweepstakes (CEDA). Of course, this also makes forensics more democratic in function and allows much greater flexibility for local programs to choose the kinds of activities and practices they are comfortable with.

The impact of this generalization is that there is little consensus about standards and practices in forensics. National organizations have helped to standardize descriptions of individual events rules and to validate some kinds of debate practices. The national organizations influence practice mainly through their influence on competitive standards. Schools may perceive, for example, that it is important to qualify for and attempt to win the national tournaments. The kinds of skills necessary to win national tournaments may not be ones appropriate for all students and all programs. Inability to compete successfully, for example, may be one major reason for a decline in participation in NDT debate during the 1980s.

National organizations have, on occasion, contributed important innovations. The NFL showcased Lincoln-Douglas as an alternative to perceived excesses in team policy debate.[12] This is the same motivation for creation of CEDA.[13] Both the NIET and NFA have dramatically expanded interest in individual events.

Despite these innovations, there is little agreement regarding educational objectives and standards for forensics. The national organizations spend most of their energy "administering" their programs rather than considering the educational ramifications of their practices. Such theorizing is usually confined to their publications or through their members participating in national conferences.

Since 1974, there have been several such conferences on forensics giving educators the opportunity to write about and discuss pedagogical issues in forensics. The Sedalia Conference (1974) established the model that most of these conferences continue to follow. The usual model is for conferences to establish working groups who draft resolutions in particular problem areas. The participants debate these resolutions in plenary sessions and vote on them. The results of the conferences are then published for distribution to the community.

These conferences have influenced the activity. The Sedalia Conference, for example, defined forensics as a "laboratory" and issued standards for the training of forensics educators. Other conferences, for both high school and college educators, have discussed the state of the activity, ethics, high school institutes, and the organizational structures of individual organizations.[14] These conferences, allowing discussion if not resolution of issues, are probably the most valuable contribution of national organizations. They help create a dialogue about important issues.

2. *Forensic practices "trickle down" from colleges to high schools.*

High school forensics is extremely decentralized in structure. Each state acts as an independent contractor. This creates a particular context where the activity lacks a coherent structure and depends on the college activity to develop theories, philosophies, and practices that eventually will be used by high school programs. Not all these changes, as we will see later, are desirable ones. The fact that high school systems reward success at high school and national tournaments, yet lack clear national guidance about desirable practices, makes them particularly susceptible to structures like summer workshops that disseminate theories and practices that might be incompatible with the educational philosophy of high school programs.

3. *Forensics is organizationally fragmented.*

As noted earlier, forensics is fragmented as a result of its lacking a coherent national voice. This has both advantages and disadvantages. The advantage is that the activity is flexible enough to allow for many organizational philosophies and structures, of which there are a variety that programs can follow. Unlike sports programs, forensics programs can more easily define themselves in ways that benefit them. They can define success as something other than "how high school X down the road is doing." Assuming the teacher is able to articulate sound educational values, this is a real advantage. Only when a teacher does not have an educational philosophy does he have to depend on artificial measures, such as comparisons with other similar schools, as the only means of justifying his program.

The downside of this phenomenon is that there is much wider room for undesirable and unethical practices to exist. No forensic organization has a code of conduct or ethics to rival that of the NCAA in college sports. While there are many ethical codes existing at both the college and high school levels, these documents lack legal power, except at national tournaments sponsored by the organization, due to the flexible nature of organizational membership. A school opposing the CEDA Code of Ethics, for example, may simply not pay its dues, thus escaping responsibility. The final chapter will return to this issue.

SUMMARY

The organizational structure of high school and college forensics is discussed in this chapter. Organizational structure is the broadest of the three systems (which will be discussed in further detail in Chapter 4) and the one that has the most significant implications for the nature of the activity. While both high school and college forensics have their own distinct organizational structures that reflect the practical and theoretical demands peculiar to each activity, there exist important interfaces between the two systems. The final section discusses the implications of organizational structure to forensic practice.

The next chapter narrows our discussion to the next system level: the forensic tournament, the place where forensic education usually occurs.

ACTIVITIES

1. Determine what organizations and leagues your school belongs to. Obtain copies, if available, of their constitutions and organizational materials. How do these materials help you to understand the philosophies and practices of the organization?

2. Discuss the organization of forensics as compared to other activities, such as athletics. Do the similarities and differences strengthen or weaken forensics? Should forensics be more tightly or more loosely organized?

NOTES

1. Brent D. Ruben and John Y. Kim (eds.), *General Systems Theory and Human Communication*. (Rochelle Park, NJ: Hayden, 1975).

2. M. McGough, "Pull It Across Your Flow." *The New Republic*, 199 (1988): 17–19. Herman Stelzner, "Tournament Debate: Emasculated Rhetoric." *Southern Speech Communication Journal*, 27 (1961): 34–42

3. Information about the NFL can be obtained from the National Office, Box 38, Ripon, WI 54791.

4. Information about the American Forensic Association can be obtained from its Executive Secretary, James Pratt, University of Wisconsin-River Falls, River Falls, WI 54022

5. Information about the Speech Communication Association can be obtained from the national office. SCA, 5105 Backlick Road, Building E., Annandale, VA 22003.

6. Information about the National Forensic Association can be obtained from the Secretary, Gerald Bluhm, Speech Communication Dept., Marshall University, Huntington, WV 25755–2633.

7. Information about CEDA can be obtained from the Executive-Secretary, Michael Bartanen, Pacific Lutheran University, Tacoma, WA 98447. Note: This is an elected position and he was the secretary in 1992.

8. Information about these honor societies can be obtained from their national offices. Membership in these fraternities is limited to schools meeting their membership qualifications.

9. Seth A. Hawkins, *Intercollegiate Speech Tournament Results*. (New Haven: Southern Connecticut State Univ.). Published yearly.

10. Pamela L. Stepp and Ralph B. Thompson, "A Survey of Forensics Activity at Selected Colleges and Universities in the United States, 1987." *National Forensic Journal*, 5 (1988): 121–136

11. There is no consensus regarding the appropriateness of hosting tournaments as a source of fund-raising. Many educators argue that tournaments should only break even and not attempt to generate significant monetary profit.

12. Richard A. Hunsaker, *Lincoln-Douglas Debate: Defining and Judging Value Debate*. (Kansas City: National Federation of State High School Assns., 1988)

13. Jack H. Howe, "CEDA's Objectives: Lest We Forget." *CEDA Yearbook 1981: The Philosophy and Practice of CEDA*.

14. The first conference was held in Sedalia, Colorado, in 1974. A second National Developmental Conference on forensics was held in Evanston, Illinois, in 1986. There have been other conferences on high school forensics, individual events, and CEDA debate in recent years.

3
Forensics as an Educational System: The Tournament

CHAPTER OVERVIEW

This chapter outlines the nature and practice of forensics tournaments, the tournament being one of the primary educational tools of forensics. The chapter explains the reason for using tournaments, as well as explaining their typical format. As the basis of forensics education, the tournament influences the nature of individual programs by forcing programs to decide on a particular tournament season and program philosophy.

The most basic systemic component of forensics is the forensic tournament, where much of the learning associated with forensics takes place. Students "gear up" to compete in tournaments in hopes of achieving their personal goals in addition to the program's goals. This chapter, while examining the tournament as an educational setting, considers the educational rationale for the tournament, its formats and practices, and the positioning of a tournament season in relation to the philosophy of a program.

THE EDUCATIONAL RATIONALE FOR THE TOURNAMENT FORMAT

Each year, there are literally thousands of high school and college tournaments held throughout the country.[1] The widespread use of the tournament as a teaching tool distinguishes forensics education in the United States from that of other nations. While there are some tournaments elsewhere (notably college tournaments in Japan), the tournament is the primary defining characteristic of U. S. forensics. The British system is the other major forensics model. The British model organizes debate around the "club" or "society." Students, as club members, occasionally debate issues in public settings instead of debating other schools in competition. This model is also used in other British Commonwealth nations and is strongly influenced by British educational practices. There is little emphasis on individual events training. The British debate model is very communication oriented so they may see little need to supplement debate with public speaking instruction.

The tournament format in forensics education is both a blessing and a curse. It is a blessing in the sense that culture in the United States heavily rewards competitive behavior, and competition is one defining characteristic of forensics in this country. We reinforce students' successfully learning debate and speaking skills by rewarding them with trophies and other visible signs of success to accompany the educational benefits that coincide. The awards are only necessary because it may take time for students to see changes in their skill and knowledge levels. Someone once remarked that debate was a "plot by English teachers to get students to go to the library." Whether true or not, the underlying sentiment is obvious: Forensics encourages students to improve their skills in speaking, reasoning, research, and aesthetic appreciation, all skills that are largely incompatible with watching television or playing video games! Competition is the engine driving the educational machine. While teachers often use debate and public speaking as classroom tools, the educational benefits are not nearly as apparent as the benefits associated with organized competitive forensics.[2] This is because forensics uses more long-term, intensive, and sustained practice in debate and speaking skills.

On the other hand, competition is also a potential drawback to forensics. This will be discussed as the ethical issues of forensics in Chapter 9. In preview of that discussion we must recognize the problems that competition presents to our educational and social systems. Some observers assert that overemphasis of competition leads to an inevitable decline in ethical standards. A case in point is "big-time" college athletics. The pressure to win at all costs leads colleges to cheat in recruiting and subvert educational and ethical values to competitive ones. Similar pressures sometimes affect forensic competition. Winning awards may cause students to circumvent ethical practices when students see the award as the end instead of the means of learning speaking and arguing skills. The teacher has a very important role in preventing misunderstanding of the proper place of awards. As discussed in Chapter 4, this is one of the reasons why teachers create a program philosophy.

THE TOURNAMENT STRUCTURE

The tournament format, as noted earlier, dates from 1923. In the early years, tournaments were very regional in makeup. Nearby schools would meet in a tournament and hold a few competitive rounds. Improvements in the national highway system expanded the ability of schools to compete in tournaments, causing the tournament format to grow in popularity. Gradually, both the number of tournaments and number of events offered at tournaments grew dramatically.

While schools might have attended 3 or 4 tournaments in the 1940s, an active college or high school program might currently attend more than 15 or 20 tournaments. Early tournaments could involve 1 or 2 debate and individual events contests and divisions. Current tournaments might offer 3 debate contests, 12 individual events contests, and possibly 3 competitive divisions. We have transformed the tournament from a simple event, easy to host, into a complex event requiring considerable preparation and not inconsiderable skill in tournament management.

HOSTING DUTIES

A tournament is an involved process requiring much preparation, tournament administration activity, and post-tournament follow-up. Figure 3.1 lists some common tasks involved in tournament administration.

Pre-Tournament Tasks

Pre-tournament tasks are necessary to bringing squads to a campus to compete. The article reproduced in Box 3.A, taken from the *Speech Communication Teacher*, gives a sample timetable for hosting a high school event.[3] A college event would be similar.

Hosts must reserve enough rooms to make sure they cover the anticipated number of rounds occurring at a particular time. They must make sure the tournament conforms to rules created by state organizations (for high school tournaments) and national organizations (for college tournaments). They then must create a tournament invitation and distribute the invitation to schools interested in attending the tournament. They must buy or print enough ballots for the tournament. The host school then has to register schools for the tournament, and create a master entry form. A master entry form shows the "school number" and the "code numbers" of the individual contestants and teams. For example:

> Pacific Lutheran - 005 [school code]
> Smith [name] 5a1 [code] Jr Expos [event]
> Kazawa & Liu [names] 5 KL [code] Intermediate CX [event]

The host also has the task of purchasing awards and finding enough guest (extra) judges to operate the tournament. Most tournaments allow schools to enter more contestants than can be covered by the judges the entering school provides, assuming they have an adequate pool of hired judges from which to draw.

FIGURE 3.1 Tasks in hosting a tournament.

Pre-tournament tasks (often beginning months prior to the event)

1. Choose a tournament date that does not conflict with other tournaments, holidays, school test days, and so on.
2. Reserve classroom space for days and times of event, including space for registration and tabulation and opening and closing assemblies.
3. Secure sanctioning for event from any or all sanctioning bodies (for example, state association).
4. Create and distribute invitations to schools who might attend. The invitation usually includes days, times, events and their descriptions, divisions, rules, entry forms, motel information, and entry fees.
5. Order debate and individual events ballots.
6. Take entries by phone or mail. Acknowledge those entries.
7. Create a master entry that lists code numbers for contestants.
8. Contact and hire extra judges.
9. Purchase trophies or awards.

Tournament administration (just prior to and during the tournament)

1. Match contestants in all divisions and events. Create posting, listing time, room, judge assignment, and contestants.
2. Register schools, providing a receipt for fees and double-checking that their entries are correct.
3. Post schedules for contestants:
4. Distribute ballots to judges.
5. Record results.
6. Power-match rounds if appropriate.
7. "Stuff" ballots, so that each contestant has all the ballots from his rounds.
8. Determine winners and award prizes.

Post-tournament activities (just after the tournament)

1. Report results if necessary.
2. Pay hired judges.

BOX 3.A Timetable for planning an invitational tournament.

6 Months Before

Arrange with activity director. Reserve building. List specific rooms to be used. Avoid conflict with SAT, ACT, PSAT dates. Contact administrator and custodian supervisor about possible costs. Assign key personnel. Delegate registration, housing, tab room, publicity, administration, transportation, refreshments, cleanup, and hospitality to student captains and parent chairpersons. Find coaches to assist in tabulation room.

3 Months Before

Prepare and print invitations. Include specific information about: events (with time limits), judging requirements, fees, deadline for mailed registration, schedule of events, directions, housing information. (Check local hotels/motels for current prices.)

10 Weeks Before

Mail invitations. Prepare advance publicity with local media, school officials, PTA. Order ballots from American Forensic Association, National Federation of State High School Associations, or print your own. Print tournament forms such as instructions to judges, housing and eating information, welcome letter, maps of school, and individual school registration forms.

8 Weeks Before

Inform teachers of rooms to be used. Ask for diagrams of room arrangements to use in cleanup. Solicit host families, if you are providing housing. Hire judges and extempore preparatory room administrator. Request extempore questions from several sources. Order trophies. Assign parents to prepare a hospitality room for judges.

7 Weeks Before

Prepare tabulation room materials: result sheets, judge and speaker cards. Pick up trophies.

continued

BOX 3.A continued

6 Weeks Before

Find student workers to be runners, tabulators, refreshment workers. Assign workers to committees.

5 Weeks Before

Prepare folders for each school, containing maps, schedules, announcements, general information. Prepare signs giving directions to rooms, designating individual events, and posting areas such as: Student Lounge, Judges' Lounge, Tabulation Room.

4 Weeks Before

Arrange supplies for tabulation room such as red and black pens, ruler, duplicating supplies, tape, paper clips, stapler, staples, 4 x 6 file cards, magic markers, construction paper, scissors, and 4 reams of paper. Make final arrangements with dietician for use of coffee urns, bowls, carts, ice, and cafeteria. Arrange with the financial secretary for cash box, change, receipt book, and method for depositing money in account.

3 Weeks Before

Record returned invitations in a predetermined filing system. Keep track of names, codes, money paid and owed. (I use a notebook because it is easy to carry with me at all times.) Assign codes to all schools and events. Duplicate registration forms with information received. Place 2 copies in the school registration folders.

2 Weeks Before

Check with all committee chairpersons about progress and problems. Assign housing requests to host families. Meet with student and parent workers to coordinate last-minute details. Request from custodians extra supplies in restrooms, a dozen plastic trash bags, and particular attention to the restrooms during the tournament. Provide administration and custodial staff with a list of all rooms to be unlocked and used. Prepare publicity coverage.

continued

BOX 3.A continued

1 Week Before

Arrange with tabulation personnel to set up first 2 rounds with random pairing, based on geography. Assign judges and rooms. Set up registration space to allow for orderly attention to correcting changed entries, collecting money, checking judges, assigning housing, and handing out the packets of information. Allow students to store their luggage in a designated place. Obtain a master key for the tournament date. Check on final details with student and parent chairpersons. Smile and enjoy during the tournament! Supervise student cleanup crews.

Week After

Turn in all money to financial secretary. Pay any remaining bills. Write thank-you letters to parents, host families, faculty, and staff.

From "Timetable for Planning an Invitational Tournament," Speech Communication Teacher. Copyright © 1988 by Speech Communication Association, Annandale, VA. Reprinted with permission.

Tournament Administration

These pre-tournament tasks are only the beginning of the hosts' responsibilities. The host usually administers the tournament. Tournament administration involves scheduling events, collecting fees, distributing ballots, recording results, collecting and "stuffing" ballots, and determining and giving awards.

Scheduling events is one difficult task in hosting a tournament. If a tournament is "randomly matched" the matcher must make sure that contestants do not compete against other contestants from their own school, or against contestants they met in an earlier round. If the tournament is "power-matched" the matcher must ensure that matches are fair. The tournament matcher also must assign judges to listen to the competition rounds. They must not assign judges to listen to the judge's own students or to hear students they have previously judged in the same event. The host also must attempt to make sure that all judges equitably share the judging load, that some people do not judge all the time and others only infrequently.

Post-Tournament Tasks

The host also must complete the various administrative tasks necessary for the tournament to operate successfully. They collect entry fees from schools entering the tournament, setting fees at a level sufficient to meet their expenses. They must gather enough supplies (such as pens, paper, file folders) to run the event. They also must distribute and collect the ballots, record the results on tabulation sheets, and return the individual ballots to the contestants and schools after the tournament. These tasks, while not individually difficult, require patience and persistence by the tournament manager to insure their successful completion. A successful tournament is the product of attending to details.

This is only a general description of all the various tasks associated with hosting a tournament. Each tournament will be different in size and complexity. For example, a high school tournament might involve as many as 70 schools and 1000 students and coaches. This may require the use of as many as 100 contest rooms for several days of competition. Other tournaments may be held in an afternoon and involve only a few schools, participants, and rooms.

There are no rules for hosting most invitational forensic tournaments. An invitational tournament is one hosted by an individual school. Tournaments hosted by state associations or college associations may have rules that govern how the event will be run. The vast majority of tournaments, however, gives the tournament host wide latitude in running the event, although there are some common guidelines about running tournaments. One such set of guidelines, making up part of the organizational Code of Ethics for the Cross-Examination Debate Association, is found at the end of this chapter. There are several books and other guidelines for hosting forensic events.[4]

EDUCATIONAL BENEFITS

While each tournament is unique, there are some general educational characteristics shared by most tournaments.

Evaluation and Criticism

Tournaments emphasize evaluation and criticism as important learning methods. Competitors are "judged" by teachers or other listeners. The judge ranks and rates the competitors compared to each other in the competitive round, and writes comments to help the speakers improve their performance. The process of judging not only fulfills competitive demands, but provides an important source of learning for the students. The students learn "audience adaptation skills." They seek feedback about the quality of their performance to increase their chances for success. The judge, if trained in communication, can encourage good speaking skills by rewarding those behaviors in the competitive speaking round through high rankings or good oral and written feedback.

Multiple Rounds of Competition

Tournaments provide multiple rounds of competition to maximize learning and minimize economic costs. The underlying assumption of the tournament model is that students should have the opportunity to practice their skills more than once. Multiple competitive rounds increase the number of other speakers a student will hear, and more importantly, increase the number of listeners critiquing the student. Multiple competitive rounds also make the tournament more cost-effective for the program to attend. Many forensics tournament costs, such as travel, meal allowances, and housing, are fixed. So it is in the program's best economic interests for students to get as much speaking opportunity as possible, in order to make scarce resources go further.

Rewards for Success

Tournaments provide rewards for success. If it is the critiques that provide the educational justification, it is the rewards that encourage students to participate in forensic activities. The awards may take several forms: public recognition, certificates, or trophies. Tournaments usually present awards and recognize winners during award assemblies.

Tournament awards are largely symbolic. Unlike Japan, where speech contest winners often receive expensive prizes, American tournaments usually give less expensive awards like trophies. Since most tournaments depend solely on the school entry fees to cover their costs, they have a limited budget for awards. Inexpensive ones also serve to reinforce the idea that the awards are less important than the educational experiences. The real award is the learning that takes place during the tournament.

Competitive Variety

Tournaments offer a variety of competitive events and levels of competition in those events. This allows many students to receive awards, based on their interest, class standing, or level of experience.

Tournaments may offer competition in either individual events or debate or a combination of both. The combination tournament (often called a "forensics" tournament, as opposed to a "debate" or "individual events" tournament) allows schools to enter students in both individual events and to debate at a single tournament. Or the school could enter some students in debate and others in individual events, allowing many students to participate in the tournament.

It is also very common for tournaments to divide contestants into divisions determined by experience level or class standing. While terms like *senior, junior,* and *novice* are often used, the definition of these divisions varies widely. Figure 3.2 shows an example of some commonly used divisions, but keep in mind that some tournaments have different definitions.

For example, CEDA, a college debate organization, defines a novice debate team as "a team where the members have less than two semesters of debate experience, including high school experience." This is more restrictive a definition than many other organizations use. State high school organizations often define eligibility standards for various divisions. Sometimes these definitions are based on the number of awards won. A novice competitor, for example, is a person who has won fewer than three awards. Other definitions base division eligibility only on class standing.

The justification for using tournament divisions is to match students of similar experience and skill in competition. Beginning students should not necessarily be matched against experienced students since they are expected to be less skilled. Similarly, students learn more from competing against students of like abilities. When competitors share similar strengths and weaknesses, they are less likely to suffer embarrassment when competing against stronger opponents.

Different divisions generally have different competitive expectations, though there are not always different rules. In debate, for instance, senior division competitors often use more sophisticated theories and arguments. In individual events, senior division competitors may use more sophisticated topics or organizational patterns.

Judges bring different expectations to critiquing senior division events than junior or novice events. They may, for example, expect the senior

FIGURE 3.2 Example of rules for determining divisions at a forensic tournament.

DIVISION	QUALIFICATIONS
Senior:	Open to anyone, or juniors or seniors.
Junior:	Open to sophomores or to juniors in their first year of competition.
Novice:	Open to contestants with no previous experience.

division competitor to have a stronger grasp of fundamental speaking or debating skills. Therefore, part of the process of adapting to a judge is for the student to learn the kinds of expectations a judge has for a competitive round in her division.

In order to be fair, high school organizations sometimes divide schools by size for the competitive purpose. Many high school state tournaments, for example, have different divisions for large, medium, and small schools, usually the same divisions that are used for sports competition. For example, Washington state, when entries warrant, divides its state tournament into a large school division and a small school division, as defined by the state association responsible for managing athletic contests.

Another way that tournaments treat students fairly is through power-matching of contestants. Power-matching is a method for deciding the placement of contestants in a competition round using previous record instead of random placement. Tournaments often use power-matching in debate, and less frequently in individual events.

There are many methods of power-matching. The theory behind power-matching schemes is matching competitors against others with the same or similar record, so the winner can be determined fairly. This equalizes competition. For example, in a power matched tournament, a debate team with a 3–0 win/loss record might be matched against another 3–0 team, instead of a team with a 0–3 record. This would presumably make the competition more equal for both the 3–0 and the 0–3 team.

Fun and Fair Play

Tournaments emphasize fun and fair play. Tournaments are exciting educational experiences. Students attend tournaments to enjoy the competition, the learning that takes place in the competitive round, and their fellow competitors. These goals require that a host administer the tournament honestly and competently so that rounds of competition happen on schedule and that all contestants have an equal chance of success.

The tournament is the main mechanism for students to improve their knowledge and skills. While much education takes place in the practice sessions before the tournament, the tournament is the primary place for students to internalize the knowledge and skills they are learning, through testing those skills in competition with others. Tournaments are defined as any form of organized competition designed for the purpose of winning awards and improving students' skills in forensic events. Tournaments involve a significant amount of advance preparation and work during the event, and while the precise nature of individual tournaments are unique, the tournament experience, in general, has shared characteristics.

THE TOURNAMENT SEASON

A tournament is both an end and a means. While considerable student and teacher energy go into being successful at a particular tournament, the individual tournament is only a part of the larger educational experience. Effective forensic education is cumulative. The student must take his experiences, critiques, and observations and use them to improve his performance at the next tournament.

It is inconceivable that a student could accomplish all possible educational objectives at a single tournament event. Effective public speaking, debate, and interpersonal interaction require people to practice, to assimilate sophisticated techniques, and to receive feedback on their efforts and level of improvement. Of course, since not every competitor can take first place, almost everyone leaves with the challenge of bettering their performance the next time.

Discussed later in the text are the particular ways that students can use a particular tournament to prepare for subsequent ones. At this point, however, the text will briefly explore the tournament season as an aspect of the forensics system.

We use the term *season* broadly. Forensic programs vary widely in the way they define a competitive season. Some programs (in both high school and college) might attend as many as 50 tournaments, while smaller programs might attend only a few. Tournaments occur mostly on weekends, although high schools often sponsor district tournaments on weekdays. The forensic season exists as both a structure and as an educational choice of the forensics program.

As a structure, the forensics season for both high schools and colleges is determined by organizational rules and the school year's limitations. The tournament season generally begins in late September and ends in April, but some states have specific rules governing its length. Washington state, for example, does not permit tournaments prior to November 1.

These are general exceptions and it is important to note that a high school or college program, with unlimited resources could undoubtedly compete every weekend between late September and early May, and then attend the national NFL high school tournament in June, and various high school workshops in July and August. It is conceivable that a forensic season could exist virtually year-round, yet such a scenario would obviously be impractical. The operational definition of the forensics season becomes a pragmatic and philosophical choice made by the forensics teacher and school. Several considerations influence the length and nature of the forensic season. These include program orientation, program size, financial support, and director availability.

Program Orientation

Program orientation refers to the competitive and educational philosophies of the program. Competitive orientation can take several forms. A *highly competitive* program attempts to be successful at either a national, regional, or state level, competing against other programs with similar orientations. A highly competitive college program usually competes nationally, attempting to be successful at national championship tournaments or in national sweepstakes competitions. A highly competitive high school program also may compete nationally (a few high school programs attend tournaments outside their state or region), but usually attempts to be successful in their own state, or in neighboring states.

The main characteristic of a highly competitive program is its level and the amount of competition. Highly competitive programs attend many tournaments and define success in winning sweepstakes awards or competing successfully at national championship tournaments. Highly competitive programs require substantial financial and coaching resources.

A second competitive orientation is a *moderately competitive* program. This program usually limits attendance to fewer tournaments overall and tournaments closer to home. A moderately competitive program defines success as occasionally winning team sweepstakes awards and being successful in national championship tournaments.

The third competitive orientation is the *modestly competitive* program. The modest program competes primarily at the local level and often involves a few students. The program may focus on achieving success at individual tournaments and be less interested in winning the state tournament or a national championship.

There should be no value judgment placed on differentiating programs in this manner. Forensics programs must orient themselves appropriately. Not every college or high school will succeed as a highly competitive program. On the other hand, programs attracting talented and motivated students will have difficulty meeting the needs of the students if they are only modestly competitive. Figure 3.3 lists some factors that the director should consider when deciding a program's orientation.

Determining a Program's Orientation

School size is one factor in determining the level of resources available. Larger schools may have more money to spend on the program and more students for a competitor pool. Larger schools may sometimes desire to support a high profile program. Or size may work the other way. The school may support so many programs that it only has limited resources to devote to any particular program.

Program orientation also depends on the second factor, the philosophy of the school, its administrators, parents, and alumni in regards to the role of a competitive program. Some colleges, for example, encourage students to study abroad or to write a senior thesis. While valuable, these may be inconsistent with sponsoring a very competitive program. Similarly, parents may want their children to participate in many events, like student government, band, and the French club. These activities also may suggest that a moderately or modestly competitive program is more appropriate.

Geography is the third factor. It is much easier to have a highly competitive program when there are many tournaments within easy travel distance. Long distance travel is both expensive and wearing on students and teachers. Long travel subtracts time from student study time and from tournament preparation.

The final factor is the personal orientation of the teacher. A teacher ought to direct a program to fit her own philosophies and teaching skills. A teacher with little background in forensics, for example, may not be a good fit in a highly competitive program. On the other hand, a teacher interested in and effective at forensics teaching may make a less competitive program more competitive.

Program Size

A second consideration influencing the nature of the forensic season is the size and quality of the forensics squad. Having more students may require more tournaments in order to provide every student with sufficient learning opportunities. Similarly, successful students, receiving positive reinforcement both educationally and competitively, often wish to compete more often. Unless taken to an extreme, this is a healthy development. The structure of forensics uniquely provides additional challenges to students. The activity provides students the chance to compete in more advanced divisions, or in more challenging competitive events.

FIGURE 3.3 Factors in program orientation.

1. *School size.* School size affects resource availability and size of the pool of potential competitors.
2. *School philosophy on competitive success.* Some schools strongly desire to be competitively successful, others may perceive participation to be more important.
3. *Geography.* The distance a school must travel to compete is a factor in how often and how successful a school can expect to be.
4. *Orientation and background of teacher.* Teachers work best in a climate they are prepared for.

Financial Resources

A third consideration influencing forensic travel is financial resources. We can divide forensic programs, like educational institutions, into "haves" and "have nots." There are extremely wide variations in forensics budgets available to both high school and college programs. While many successful programs operate on shoestrings, richer programs are able to attend more tournaments. This does not mean they are always more successful. Competitive success is determined by several interrelating factors, of which only one is money.

Teaching Orientation and Preparation

Finally, and certainly not least in order of importance in determining the competitive season, is the readiness of the teacher. Even if forensics was a teacher's only professional responsibility, the sheer length of the season would prove to be extremely debilitating.

As we will see in the next chapter, directing a program is not simply a weekend activity, but a job that takes many hours. Traveling to tournaments takes away from both personal time and other professional activities. The forensics teacher must select a season that allows her to balance the competitive and educational needs of the students with her own needs. A professional problem forensics educators face is this balancing act, particularly when the director does not have control over determining the season or acquiring assistance in travel and teaching.

SUMMARY

The tournament is an important educational system. The tournament experience provides much of the motivation for students to prepare and compete. The individual tournament is (1) a complex entity, involving extensive preparation and planning, and (2) is part of a larger system, the forensics season. The forensics season exists to take advantage of the cumulative nature of forensics education, where students gradually become more proficient at various skills and behaviors. The forensics season is both a structure and a philosophical decision.

The next chapter completes a systemic description of forensics by focusing on the forensics program as an interpersonal and organizational system.

ACTIVITIES

1. Attend a forensics tournament on your campus or at a nearby high school or college. Observe how it is organized. Identify as many hosting and administrative tasks as you can. How many of these tasks are evident to the students attending the tournament?

2. Discuss with a high school or college forensics teacher his program philosophy and approach to the tournament season. What factors does he identify as significant to his tournament and season choices? Is his program philosophy consistent with his personal philosophy of the activity?

NOTES

1. There are no statistics on the number of high school tournaments. College tournament results are reported in a publication, *Intercollegiate Speech Tournament Results*, edited (1992) by Seth Hawkins, Southern Connecticut State University.

2. The benefits of forensics were discussed in Chapter 1.

3. "Timetable for Planning an Invitational Tournament," *Speech Communication Teacher*, Winter, 1989, p. 7.

4. W. Brown and P. Swisher, *Directing Successful Speech Tournaments*. (Grandview: Dale Publishing, 1980). G. T. Goodnight and D. Zarefsky, *Forensics Tournaments: Planning and Administration*. (Lincolnwood: National Textbook, 1980).

APPENDIX TO CHAPTER 3

CEDA Tournament
Administration Principles (1992)

The Cross-Examination Debate Association (CEDA) has specified some guiding principles as part of their Code of Ethics. You will find additional tournament standards contained in the Code of Ethics of the American Forensic Association, which is appended to Chapter 9.

IV. Tournament administration

In administering tournaments, educators should strive to ensure that all students have an equal opportunity to excel. Educators should be particularly cognizant of the issues involved in scheduling and judge assignment. Tournament administration should seek to promote high quality and fair learning experiences for all debaters. Tournaments should be hosted for educational, not profit-making, reasons.

A. In order to give all participants equal information about tournament procedures, tournament invitations should include clear definitions of events and divisions, clear explanations of matching and judge assignment systems, clear explanations of criteria for advancement to elimination rounds and for awards, clear announcements of fees and schedules, and a clear statement of tournament rules.

B. In order to provide a fair and educational tournament, administrators matching debate rounds should attempt to allow students an equal number of rounds on each side of the resolution and should maximize insofar as possible the range of opponents encountered by each team.

C. In order to provide a fair and educational tournament, judge assignment insofar as possible should be random. Debaters should have equal opportunity to be heard by a range of judges and to be protected from judges who might have a conflict of interest.

D. In order to maximize the educational function of tournaments, administrators should make results and ballots available to all participants as soon as possible at the end of competition.

APPENDIX ON TOURNAMENT ADMINISTRATION

Many items related to tournament administration are not ethical issues. Furthermore, except for provisions contained in By-laws II and III of the CEDA Constitution, the Cross-Examination Debate Association leaves tournament administration procedures to local hosts. In order to assist students and coaches who seek information about tournament procedures, this appendix sets forth some guidelines that typify the operations of many debate tournaments.

I. Guidelines for debate tournament matching that protect equality of competition include:
   A. A debate team should not meet the same team during preliminary rounds of a tournament unless:
      1. There are so few teams entered that it would be impossible for the tournament to proceed, in which case the two teams should switch sides the second time they meet, or
      2. The schools entering the tournament have agreed to suspend the provision that teams not debate each other twice in preliminary rounds.
   B. So far as possible, debate teams should debate an equal number of preliminary rounds on each side of the debate proposition. Rounds on each side of the question should generally alternate. In tournaments with an odd number of preliminary rounds, efforts should be made to balance a team's total of affirmative and negative contests when matching even numbered rounds.
   C. Tournament round matching procedures should be advertised in the invitation to include:
      1. The number of rounds pre-set with the principles guiding pre-set assignment (i.e., "random," "geographic distribution," "approximate strength of schedule," etc.).
      2. The number of power matched rounds and principles guiding power-matching (i.e., "high-low," "high-high," "lag-power," etc.).
II. Guidelines for judge assignment that protect equality of competition include:
   A. A judge should not be assigned to judge his/her own team.
   B. A judge should not judge the same debate team twice during a tournament's preliminary rounds unless there is no way to avoid this conflict. In such cases, the judge should hear the debate team on the opposite side, unless it is impossible to do this, or the schools competing agree to suspend this provision.
   C. A judge should not judge the same debate team in elimination rounds that s/he has previously heard in the preliminary rounds or in successive elimination rounds if it can be avoided.

D. A judge should not judge debaters when there is a conflict of interest possible, such as:

1. The judge has previously coached in college a debater s/he is to hear.

2. The judge was, within the last two years, the coach of the school whose team s/he is about to hear.

3. The judge was, within the last two years, an undergraduate forensics competitor at the school whose team s/he is about to hear.

E. Prior to the start of the tournament, all judges should have the opportunity to declare themselves ineligible to hear specific debate teams due to conflict of interest.

F. The practice of allowing debate teams to prevent a specific judge from hearing a particular team should be permitted only when:

1. All teams are given an equal chance to declare judge strikes prior to the start of the tournament.

2. All teams are granted the same number of strikes.

3. Once a judge is struck, s/he should not be assigned to judge those teams who struck him/her at any time during the tournament. Any procedures for removing strikes should be stated openly to all competitors.

III. Guidelines for tournament invitations that promote fair competition should include:

A. Specification of the level of competition expected (i.e., "Open," "Novice," "Lincoln-Douglas," etc.).

B. Clear definitions of all divisions of competition.

C. Explanation of the basis of advancing competitors to the elimination rounds and for determining awards:

1. For advancing teams to elimination rounds it is assumed the win-loss record is the first criterion. Beyond win-loss criterion, tournaments should specify the order of subordinate criteria (i.e., team points, adjusted team points, opposition record, etc.).

2. For determining speaker awards, invitations should specify the criteria for determining awards (i.e., speaker points, adjusted speaker points, ranks, etc.).

D. Explanation of the basis for assigning sweepstakes points if awarded.

E. Statement of time limits for all events including preparation time (if used).

F. Explanation of judge assignment procedures used (i.e., "random," "power," etc.). Invitations should indicate whether a judge preference/strike system will be used.

G. Announcement of tab room staff and personnel if not from the host school. Invitations should note if a computer package is used to administer a tournament.

H. Explanation of the nature of the anticipated judging pool (i.e., "attorneys," "lay persons," etc.).

I. Indication of whether results are to be kept secret.

J. Indication of whether the hold school is eligible to receive awards or participate in elimination rounds.

IV. Guidelines for general tournament administration practices include:

A. Tournament directors should ensure that results and ballots are made available to all contestants as soon as possible at the end of the competition.

B. Tournaments should not be designed to operate at a personal profit to any individual.

C. Tournaments should run smoothly and efficiently with schedules realistically allowing:

1. Time for judges to complete their ballots;

2. Meal breaks at appropriate hours;

3. Power-matching (it is recommended that, whenever possible, power-matching occur at the end of the day or during meal breaks); and

4. Beginning and ending times that allow competitors and judges to rest.

4
Forensics as an Interpersonal and Organizational System: The Program

CHAPTER OVERVIEW

A forensics program is more than simply students and a teacher preparing for and competing in tournaments. A program consists of a number of activities and subsystems. There are three domains in a program: (1) the interpersonal domain, or the systems connected with dealing with interpersonal issues; (2) the organizational domain, or those systems concerned with managing the program; and (3) the educational domain, or the teaching that takes place. This chapter outlines the activities connected with the interpersonal and organizational domains.

The heart of forensics is the program, for it is the program that defines the educational philosophies and competitive values that shape the kind of experience the student receives through participating in forensics. The program is the point of reference the student uses to judge whether her experience was meaningful to her in both the short and long term. If she is uncomfortable with the organizational climate of the program, she is not likely to participate for long or support the program after finishing competition. Like any complex organization, a forensics program is not simply a group of students participating in a shared endeavor: It is a system with formal organizational structures, a definable interpersonal climate, and definite inputs, throughputs, and outputs.

The discussion of the forensics program in this chapter as an interpersonal and organizational system will be necessarily broad. There is no prototypical forensics program. Each program shares some general characteristics but remains unique. A program is unique because it is only a part of the broader organizational climate of its sponsoring school, and each school has different bureaucratic structures and educational values. The teacher's first task is understanding the unique nature of the school in order to understand the relationship of the forensics program to the school.

Assuming there is only one kind of program is foolhardy. A program must exist compatibly with all other systems that influence it.

Programs that do not fit with surrounding systems will not flourish and may not survive. For example, increasing numbers of both high school and college students work part time. A program philosophy requiring significant advanced tournament preparation that does not account for the time and pressures of part-time jobs will not likely keep many students. Similarly, as noted in Chapter 3, certain program philosophies (for example, being highly competitive) require both money and teaching resources. Unless the school is willing to fulfill these needs, such a program philosophy cannot work and will likely create unhappiness for students, teachers, and the school itself.

As stated before, while each program is unique, they share some program elements. Figure 4.1 diagrams the general nature of the forensics program.

As an organizational and interpersonal system, a forensics program includes three domains. A domain includes major activities grouped under a central purpose. Each domain contains two subsystems, which include the specific activities required to accomplish the program's purposes.

The first domain is the interpersonal dimension of a program. A program in one sense consists of interpersonal relationships between teachers, students, and competitors. Recruitment is the subsystem for finding and keeping students in the program. The interpersonal relationships subsystem describes the communication climate present and the factors influencing the relationships among all the people involved in the program.

The second domain is the organizational dimension of the program. A program is also an organization that consists of formal relationships, rules, and interactions. Financing/management is the subsystem for completing the activities (such as attending tournaments) connected with forensics. The justification/public relations subsystem describes how the director presents, explains, and justifies the program.

FIGURE 4.1 The parts of a forensics program.

THE FORENSIC PROGRAM

INTERPERSONAL DOMAIN
- Recruiting students
- Managing interpersonal relationships

ORGANIZATIONAL DOMAIN
- Financing and management of program
- Justification and public relations

EDUCATIONAL DOMAIN
- Teaching and coaching
- Teaching and judging

The third domain is the educational domain, where the actual interaction between student and teacher occurs. This interaction takes the form of (1) the teaching/coaching subsystem, in which the teacher helps the student prepare for competition, and (2) the teaching/judging subsystem, in which the teacher assists other students to learn through criticism during the actual event.

Each of these program domains and subsystems are interrelated. Changes in one affects the others. Poor recruitment, for example, may make it difficult to justify the program or raise money. Creating a positive learning environment may justify more funding for the program and help recruit more students. In each program you will find that these domains and subsystems differ in their interrelations.

Administering any forensics program consists of performing activities connected with these domains. Each program is unique in how much time and energy the teacher devotes to a particular domain. One program, for example, may spend little time recruiting students, but considerable time justifying itself to the educational system. A new program, on the other hand, may spend significant time recruiting students. Learning about the particular educational environment of his school will help the teacher decide how much attention a domain or subsystem needs at any particular time.

The rest of this chapter examines the interpersonal and organizational domains and sketches the subsystems that cover the activities in those areas. Chapters 5, 6, and 7 consider the forensics program as an educational domain. As an educational system, teaching and learning activities are the most important systems elements so they are examined in more detail.

THE INTERPERSONAL DOMAIN

The first domain consists of the interpersonal elements of the forensics program. Stripped of all other aspects, the basic units of forensics are people and relationships. A program may have very sound organizational and educational domains, but lacking the ability effectively to recruit, motivate, and relate to students will be educationally unsuccessful and unproductive. The two subsystems of the interpersonal domain are recruitment of students and the handling of interpersonal relationships.

Recruiting Students

Students have many competing priorities. High school students involve themselves in many activities to discover their interests or to prepare for college. They also may work part time to earn spending or college money.

College students often hold down a job while studying and actively participating in social or other college activities. In addition, people sometimes perceive forensics stereotypically as an activity only for "smart people." These commitments, added to the allure of television and video games, can make attracting students to participate in forensics a challenge, despite its obvious benefits.

Recruiting students to participate in forensics depends on understanding the reasons why forensics attracts students, then finding ways to use those sources of attraction. Forensics attracts students for many reasons.

1. *Students perceive forensics as valuable career and educational preparation.* This remains the primary reason why students participate in the activity. Teachers traditionally advocate forensics as preparation for law school. While this remains a strong belief, forensics supporters have broadened this appeal to include suggesting that forensics is sound preparation for many other careers such as politics, education, business and even the sciences.[1]

2. *Students perceive forensics as a way to learn public speaking.* Communication anxiety is remarkably widespread in the United States. As many as 5 percent of Americans suffer from moderate to high anxiety levels when facing the possibility of public speaking. Modest anxiety levels are even more widespread for virtually anyone without public speaking training. A strong selling point of forensics is its value in training students in public speaking.

While people with severe communication anxiety may not benefit from forensics (since the competitive element probably would exacerbate their fears), those with moderate or slight anxiety can profit. Since competitive speeches can be perceived as both nonthreatening (no grade is given) and fun, students can be encouraged to confront and overcome their fears. Tournaments often group forensics competitors by age or experience. Inexperienced students most often compete in contexts where they share their anxieties and are judged against other inexperienced students. The tournament model also usually encourages judges to support inexperienced speakers by providing written (and sometimes oral) feedback designed to reinforce good skills and overcome weaknesses.

3. *Students perceive forensics as fun.* Any forensics model that minimizes the enjoyable nature of the activity is misdirected. Learning theories have always stressed the importance of enjoyment in learning. Even if students understand the educational benefits of the activity, they are unlikely to participate unless they perceive potential personal rewards, making participation "cost-beneficial."[2]

4. *Students perceive forensics as a way to meet and share experiences with interesting people.* Besides having fun, people participate in forensics to meet other people with whom they share common interests. The interpersonal dimension is a significant factor in motivating student behavior. People are attracted to situations where they perceive they will find other like individuals.[3] This motivation is particularly strong for younger people. High school students often strongly identify with people they admire or with whom they share interests. College students often need to form relationships to replace ones lost when they leave home for the unknown college world. In both instances, forensics provides individuals the benefit of forming relationships with advanced knowledge that those they meet will share at least one common interest. This makes the process of forming the relationship that much easier.

Successfully recruiting students depends on combining these motivations with well-known public relations techniques. There is no substantive difference between recruiting forensics students and any other form of recruitment or sales. There are several techniques that can be used.[4]

1. *Use word-of-mouth recruitment.* Word-of-mouth may be the best way to recruit students. Students who enjoy their experience will naturally attract other students. Since we are attracted to people that have similar interests, this need conveniently provides the program with students who fit with the program's philosophy.

2. *Be publicly visible.* Public performances of debates or speeches are a valuable way of recruiting students. Watching students perform attracts students by giving recruits role models and insight into their own improvement and enjoyment. A high school program, for example, might give public demonstrations to middle schools. A college program might give demonstrations to local high schools. The key in each instance is to stress the personal benefits and enjoyment associated with forensics competition.

3. *Use personal contacts.* Personal relationships may outweigh other factors in the decision to attend one college over another. Knowing this, college sports recruiters rely heavily on personal conversations with potential recruits. Similarly, a student may decide to participate in forensics because they like the teacher or the students in the program. Students may relish the chance to have a close relationship with a teacher or professor. As your own experience may confirm, both high schools and colleges can be places where students have few opportunities to work closely with instructors. Forensics can be a way of filling the need for close work with a mentor.

Handling Interpersonal Communication

The second subsystem of the interpersonal domain consists of managing relationships. The perception that relational dimensions of an organization can influence organizational success and well being is not, of course, a new idea. Douglas McGregor discussed the "human dimension" of organizational success in the 1960s.[5] More recently, Paul Watzlawick and his associates sketched the dual nature of "content" and "relational" dimensions of communicative behavior.[6] The duality of content and relationship is central to many contemporary communication theories.

This perspective argues that content and relationship are intertwined in communication. Since any message has both a simultaneous content and relationship dimension, the message can only be properly understood by looking at both parts. This insight led Watzlawick to develop axioms of communication ("One cannot not communicate") that enriched our understanding of the complexity of the communicative process.

Many theorists have developed similar insights into organizational behavior. Organizations, they argue, have "cultures" and "climates" that strongly influence behaviors. These cultures may not be planned or even controlled, but the relational climate and organizational culture have a clear link to organizational success.[7] Contemporary interest in Japanese theories of management is an example of this linkage.

Although the Japanese organizational culture has its own weaknesses, the Japanese model illustrates the interconnection of relationships and outputs. Japanese workers often have a much stronger stake in the internal workings and ultimate success of the organization than do workers in the United States. Japanese companies, through institutional structures such as *karaoke* and *quality circles*, create an organizational climate that encourages the belief that the worker and the organization are interrelated.[8]

Relational factors are also significant in organizational outputs in forensics programs. The forensics teacher is likely to spend a considerable amount of time managing relationships and other interpersonal issues. The importance of creating and maintaining an appropriate communication climate is, perhaps, the one constant of all forensics programs.

Communication Climate

Communication climate refers to the communicative atmosphere that exists. A climate where students feel comfortable and unthreatened (such as the one created by Robin Williams's character in the movie *Dead Poets Society*) makes a classroom very different from the confrontational atmosphere found in some law schools and other settings (as characterized by John Houseman as Professor Kingsfield in the movie *The Paper Chase*). This latter climate is coming under increasing criticism as one that is not compatible with effective education. An educational climate creating stress and confrontation may not encourage effective retention or a desire to learn.

The dichotomy between these two educational climates is even more significant in forensics education. Forensics education works best with a supportive climate that stresses cooperation over confrontation. There are several reasons supporting this belief.

First, forensic activities require substantial ego-involvement. Public performance of debates or speeches involves significant risk-taking behavior by participants. A student performing publicly takes a risk that she will not be well received by the listener. Good speeches require personal commitment and involvement. This can make student egos fragile, since the tournament format constantly subjects them to negative and positive criticism. A speech or debate is unlikely to be perfect. The less experienced the student the further she is likely to be from perfection. This can create dissonance for the student as she deals with the gap between the ideal and the reality of her performance.

The student may wrongly perceive that a negative comment about her speech is really a comment denigrating her self-worth. While the difference between the two interpretations is intuitively obvious, it is an extremely difficult distinction for students to draw during the "heat of the battle." The teacher must constantly monitor this relational dimension and help students recognize the difference between comments about the content of their speeches and judgments about the self-worth of the speaker.

Second, forensic activities often involve close cooperative interaction with others. Sometimes there is the misapprehension about forensics that it is an activity solely for loners who hang out by themselves in the library. This myth is hardly ever borne out by experience. Competitive forensics combines elements of both team and individual activities. While the most basic forensic activities are individualized (a speaker writes and delivers a speech himself) there is considerable dyadic and group interaction that takes place.

Avoiding Interpersonal Conflict

The dyadic interaction occurs when students combine their efforts with others to make up a debate team, duo-interpretation team, or even to work together on individual speeches or debate preparations. Whenever two individuals work together there is the potential for misunderstanding or even conflict. The conflict may come from clashing egos, disagreements about strategies or content, or from sources extraneous to forensics. The individuals may have only limited experience in cooperative situations and may not be comfortable in working through the conflict symptoms. Interpersonal conflict may be a great challenge for the forensics teacher. There are several conclusions we can draw about the special nature of conflict in forensics.

1. *It is unlikely that "people do not have to like each other to work together productively."*

There is a persistent misbelief that task productivity can occur even when individuals do not like those with whom they are working. This might be true in some limited instances. However, there is a relationship between the ability of people to get along with each other and their working success. This seems true up to the point where the relationship itself replaces the task in order of importance to the individuals.

This does not imply that partners have to be best buddies. Modest levels of conflict and disagreement help both the development of the relationship and the accomplishment of the task. Too close a relationship may be harmful as it may prevent individuals from offering helpful criticism to each other, and may cause them to spend time on their social relationship that might be better spent on their preparation.

In these instances, the teacher must discuss the implications of the closeness of the relationship on the students' ability to work together. As happens when students are not doing so, the teacher's first role is to attempt mediation. The teacher should try to help the students work through their conflict through honest discussion. If that solution fails the teacher may need to take more drastic steps. They may have to break up their partnership, or find ways for both people to work independently of each other. If conflict continues, the teacher may need to ask one or both individuals to leave the team.

2. *Interpersonal conflict is inevitable but not necessarily harmful.*

Contemporary theory is consistent in arguing that conflict is an ever-present part of relationships. This is particularly true in forensics programs. There is much disappointment and frustration that inevitably accompanies competition. Students often are frustrated and disappointed that they were not more successful. They sometimes take out that frustration on themselves and each other, without always directing their anger at the right person or object.

Anger and conflict are undesirable when they are manifest in unproductive ways. Some unproductive behaviors include

- Publicly berating a team member or judge after a contest
- Blaming others unjustifiably for instances of lacking success
- Using physical or emotional violence
- Failing to take responsibility for personal actions and behaviors
- Brooding and internalizing situations, allowing them to fester and worsen

These behaviors are not unique to forensics. Baseball players throw bats and kick dirt on umpires among other unproductive conflict behaviors. Forensics, as an educational activity, tries to discourage these unproductive behaviors. As part of their education students ought to use the ups and downs of forensics to learn appropriate conflict strategies

3. *Forensic activities often stimulate unproductive competitive strategies.*

The third and final justification for developing a supportive environment in forensics programs is as a partial antidote to harms associated with excessive competition.

A more comprehensive discussion of the role of competition is better left to a wider analysis of ethics that will come in Chapter 9. It is important to examine the interpersonal dimension of competition at this point. Competitiveness is, after all, a behavioral dimension that is possibly unique to human beings. In this sense, competitiveness must be separated from the survival instinct of other living things. Interpersonal competitiveness refers to situations where individuals are actively seeking scarce resources and perceive that the outcome probably will be a "zero-sum" game.[9]

Competitiveness can be both helpful and harmful in forensics. It can be helpful in the sense that competition for awards and success may motivate people to learn ideas and skills they might not otherwise learn. Because there is no clear dividing line between appropriate and inappropriate competitiveness, it can be harmful. Sometimes it is difficult to channel competitiveness into appropriate directions.

This too is a dilemma of a larger society that often rewards competitive behaviors no matter their ethical or social consequences. The virtual mystification of the phrase attributed to the late Vince Lombardi, "winning isn't everything, it's the only thing," is an example of the societal uncertainty about competition. People cheer for winners while simultaneously castigating "Little League Parents" and others displaying undesirable competitive behaviors.

There is obviously no single correct perspective about competition. It is important, however, for the forensics teacher to be aware of the nature and consequences of competitiveness. They should actively engage the student in developing an ethical perspective about competition that fits into the educational aim of the forensics program.

In summary, the interpersonal domain of forensics programs consists of the tasks of recruiting students and managing interpersonal relationships of the participants.

THE ORGANIZATIONAL DOMAIN

The second major domain consists of the organizational elements of the program. The forensics teacher, besides teaching public speaking and debate skills, must also spend considerable time administering the program. This administration takes two forms—financing/management and justification/public relations.

Financing/Management

Program administration is time-consuming, often difficult, and personally unrewarding, but integral to the health and success of the program. The forensics teacher will spend literally hundreds of hours on administrative tasks that detract from the time available to work directly with students. This can cause frustration and burnout. Lax attention to administrative details also can be harmful. At the very least, it may lead to wasting precious resources. In the worst case, improper administration may cause job loss or legal difficulties. The increasing litigious climate of contemporary society has increased the care that forensics directors must take in administering their programs.

While few forensics teachers enjoy the administrative burdens, most learn to cope with it. They find ways of efficiently running their programs to free up more teaching time. Figure 4.2 lists some administrative responsibilities commonly associated with forensics teaching.

The chart shows the diverse administrative responsibilities of the forensics teacher. While each teaching position is a little different, these three administrative areas are common.

Budget Administration

The first area is budget administration. The forensics director is usually directly responsible for administering the program budget. The budget itself could be one or more accounts covering items such as tournament travel, entry fees, materials, and so on. The entire forensics budget may be as small as a few hundred dollars in a high school, or as much as seventy-five thousand dollars in a large university.

Schools and universities have created increasingly complex procedures for spending money. This is motivated by the desire to stretch scarce dollars and the need to meet the requirements of fiscal auditors. In earlier times, forensics programs operated on the "honor system" in which the directors withdrew however much money they needed and were not asked to document expenses. Virtually no school operates on that principle today. Instead, the director may be called on to seek a travel advance by documenting anticipated expenses. He will justify that advance at the conclusion of the trip with receipts for each dollar spent.

FIGURE 4.2 Administrative responsibilities of forensics teachers.

BUDGET ADMINISTRATION
1. Seeking and justifying a program budget.
2. Short- and long-range planning of spending.
3. Understanding and complying with internal budgeting and financial procedures.

TRIP ADMINISTRATION
1. Securing transportation to the tournament.
2. Making housing reservations.
3. Understanding and complying with tournament rules and entry procedures.
4. Coordinating travel plans with students' school and work schedules.
5. Supervising students on the trip.

PERSONNEL ADMINISTRATION
1. Securing judges or coaches as needed.
2. Training judges and coaches about both philosophy and process.

PROGRAM ADMINISTRATION
1. Creating and distributing a program philosophy.
2. Ensuring that a program is administered in a legally correct manner.

In addition, there may be rules guiding how money may or may not be spent. This is particularly true in some public school and university systems, where rules govern spending student money on teachers, or spending money on lodging or food.

While administering the budget is probably not much more difficult than balancing a checkbook, it is a skill requiring some practice. A new forensics director must familiarize herself with the particular financial process at the school. She must engage in long-range planning to divide the budget among all tournaments and activities the program will engage in. The teacher should not ignore these administrative issues.

Administrative issues are both pragmatic and philosophical. The pragmatic issues are fairly straightforward. The forensics director must spend the budget appropriately. The philosophical issues are less clear—they relate to (1) matching the budget with the program philosophy, and (2) choosing whether to spend the director's own money or the students' money to attend tournaments.

When matching the budget to the program philosophy, there is a temptation, if resources are tight, to prioritize spending toward the more talented students at the expense of inexperienced competitors. There is no precise formula regarding how the director should resolve this problem. The only guidance comes from the philosophy of the program. The students should understand the program philosophy about spending money. One useful way of communicating the philosophy is through creating a squad handbook outlining the program philosophy and rules. This handbook should include information about how resources will be spent. It might address questions such as:

1. What are the criteria the director uses for selecting people to attend tournaments?
2. Is tournament attendance determined by experience or other criteria?
3. Does the amount of work a student does influence their chances to travel?

The question of whether a teacher ought to subsidize his program with his own money is important. Both college and high school teachers are underpaid, yet there is the temptation to stretch budget dollars by spending money out-of-pocket for some expenses. The teacher, for instance, may choose not to pay for his own food or lodging with school funds in order to stretch the forensics budget. While tempting, spending money out-of-pocket is a bad precedent. It allows the school to avoid the responsibility to fund a program adequately. It also puts the teacher in a problematic position if questions about spending school money arise.

Another administrative problem a forensics director must often address is whether it is appropriate for students to pay part of their own expenses while competing in forensics tournaments. This is both a philosophical and pragmatic problem. The philosophical side of the problem considers whether forensics competition ought to be reserved for those who can afford to participate. Would competitor-subsidized competition prevent students from competing? Would wealthy students have more opportunities than students from modest means? These are philosophical questions that must be answered in terms of the school and program philosophy.

The pragmatic issue becomes the decision of how much the competitors should subsidize and whether the subsidies conflict with school financial policies. For example, if students supply their own transportation to a tournament, is the school or teacher liable for injury in an accident?

Trip Administration

The second administrative area is trip administration. Like planning a family vacation, forensics travel takes some advanced preparation for things to go smoothly. Usually, the forensics teacher is responsible for these activities.

The teacher will need to arrange transportation, housing, and tournament entry. Many schools have buses or vans that can be reserved for use. Often these vehicles must be reserved well ahead of the anticipated trip. If air travel is anticipated, lower fares can be found for advance purchase. Similarly, the teacher will need to reserve hotel or other accommodations at the tournament. Finding reasonably priced lodging is an art rather than a science and may take persistence and many telephone calls!

The teacher also will need to enter the tournament in whatever manner (telephone, mail, or fax) the tournament invitation specifies. The teacher will need to decide in what events and divisions she will enter contestants, based on the students' level of preparation and experience. If necessary, the teacher will need to find sufficient judges to cover her entry in the tournament. The teacher will need to brief the students on the schedule and process for competing in the tournament. She also will need to decide how much entry fees they owe and prepare to pay the entry fee at the time of registration for the tournament.

The teacher also will need to supervise the students at the tournament. This involves scheduling meal times, transporting students to, from, and during the tournament, and supervising them during the evenings if the tournament involves overnight stays. The teacher may need to cope with unexpected events like illness or accident, and the demanding interpersonal problems associated with the tournament experience.

Personnel Administration

The third administrative area is personnel administration. As noted previously, the teacher may need to find, train, and supervise extra judges or coaches for the program. Often these extra judges may have only limited experience in forensics judging and little exposure to the philosophy of the forensics program. The teacher is responsible for recruiting these people and training them sufficiently to become good educators while they are judging.

This recruiting often occurs before the actual tournament. For example, the high school teacher may recruit some parents to judge at an upcoming tournament. The teacher must then instruct the parents on the essentials of judging and give them a philosophy of judging that is consistent with the program philosophy.

Program Administration

The last aspect of program administration that the director must consider is administering the program in a legally correct manner. Directing a forensics program may subject the teacher to potential legal actions. Negligence in driving a car full of students, negligence or malfeasance in supervising students, and improper behaviors with students are three examples of potential legal difficulties that could arise from directing a forensics program.

Fortunately, there are relatively few instances of legal problems arising from a teacher's forensics activities. Those which have occurred have been mainly through automobile accidents. Most schools do provide the teacher with legal protection for the teacher's actions, assuming the teacher acts appropriately. The forensics teacher should, however, take steps to protect his legal rights. Professor Sharon Porter and attorney Martin Sommerness recommend: (1) The teacher should understand his contract with the university, and what legal implications his actions might have. (2) The teacher should purchase the maximum amount of insurance available. If the teacher does not have sufficient coverage through his regular insurance, he should increase his coverage with a supplemental policy. (3) The teacher should publish travel rules and procedures. This could be a part of the squad handbook. (4) The teacher should obtain releases from students before each trip. Such releases should be prepared with appropriate administrators. (5) The director should obtain authorizations for medical treatments for students. (6) The teacher should be proactive, keeping up on changes in the law and school policies. (7) The teacher should use common sense in his actions.[10]

Common sense is wise advice for most aspects of program administration. Safely traveling, closely supervising students, and being prepared for medical or other emergencies are very important precautions that teachers ought to take to avoid unduly exposing themselves to potential legal problems.

In summary, being a forensics teacher means that a person is part chauffeur, bookkeeper, travel agent, financial planner, baby-sitter, tour guide, and recruiter. The competing demands of these positions are often difficult to keep balanced with the desire to spend all available time working directly with students.

Justification/Public Relations

The second subsystem of the organizational domain of the forensics program is programmatic justification and other public relations activities. This domain receives the least attention in the forensics pedagogy literature. It is often erroneously believed to be strictly ancillary to the forensic teacher's other activities. In actuality, this domain is very important to the success and well being of the forensics program.

Public relations refers to the process of explaining or defending an organization and its actions to other people. Most organizations regularly conduct systematic public relations activities. Large organizations have sophisticated PR efforts involving many individuals in the process. Small organizations may do nothing more than tell the local newspaper their meeting times. In either case, effective public relations efforts are a significant part of organizational success.

Forensics is often a publicly invisible activity in either a college or high school. Forensics tournaments are not public spectacles like sports events. Most of the teaching and learning happens in late afternoon or evening, after classes are over. This usually means that people outside the activity do not properly understand or appreciate the learning taking place.

The implications of programmatic invisibility are often significant. Less visible programs often receive less financial and other forms of support. This is not due to spite as much as the realities of politics. In any political system, administrators are reluctant to cut back programs that are visible or perceived as essential. Decision-makers perceive such programs, correctly or not, as more defensible. When cutbacks need to occur, or when resources for expanding programs are available, administrative perceptions of programs can be pivotal.

Good public relations efforts are also philosophically important. Visibility is a form of student and faculty reward. Student athletes, speakers, and artists value support from their peers. This support helps to reinforce the educational values of those activities. Good public relations also helps to recruit new participants and to justify the activity to the public.

Public relations for the forensics program usually is unlike similar activities conducted for athletic programs or corporations. Time constraints prevent forensics teachers being the equivalent of "sports information directors." Furthermore, media usually do not perceive the forensics program to be newsworthy. There are some specific public relations activities that increase visibility of the program without detracting from other important teaching duties.

1. *Prepare and distribute regular press releases.* Part of the answer to increasing public visibility is to provide usable information to school or university public relations agencies or to the news media. Providing the information in the same press release form that these groups use may increase the likelihood of receiving coverage. (See the appendix at the end of this chapter for an example of a press release.)

2. *Attempt to persuade student media to cover forensics as a beat.* Usually, student media justify their existence by claiming to cover newsworthy items at school or on campus. Sending press releases to the student media and trying to encourage the media to assign the forensics beat to a reporter may increase visibility and recruitment.

3. *Maintain alumni contact.* Alumni are an excellent resource for both high school and college programs. They may be a source of fund-raising, judging, recruitment, or simply public support. The advantage of communicating with alumni is that they understand the nature of the activity. It is

not necessary to educate them about the nature of or rationale for competitive events. Alumni contact may take the form of newsletters, homecoming receptions, or even brief articles in alumni publications.

4. *Hold public speech events.* Consider holding a public event where students perform their speeches or a public debate. These events increase public visibility and teach valuable audience adaptation skills.

5. *End the year with a banquet.* At this banquet, you could give out squad awards, initiate students in the speech fraternity (if the school belongs), or simply celebrate the forensics season. These banquets are an excellent opportunity to invite family, alumni, administrators, and others to acknowledge publicly the efforts of the forensics students.

While a banquet may be costly it does not have to be an elaborate event to accomplish its purpose. The banquet might be held, if appropriate, in a school cafeteria or some other informal location.

SUMMARY

This chapter examines the forensics program as an interpersonal and organizational system. This system is made up of three domains: interpersonal, organizational, and educational. The interpersonal domain consists of activities associated with working with individual students and meeting their competitive and personal needs. The organizational domain consists of the administrative and public relations responsibilities of the program as part of larger organizational needs. The next three chapters describe the educational domain, or the teaching elements of the forensics program.

ACTIVITIES

1. Briefly outline a program philosophy that you might use in either a college or a high school program. Discuss your outline with others to identify strengths and weaknesses in your approach. If possible, compare your philosophy with a philosophy used in an existing program.

2. Interview athletic coaches, music teachers, or other school figures who are involved with public programs. How do they handle interpersonal, administrative, and public relations details? Have they found any short cuts or suggestions about handling these details efficiently?

3. Find out what administrative regulations (for spending money, supervising students, and so on) are followed by your school. Are those regulations easy enough to understand and follow? Create a list of questions you may need to ask for clarification of those regulations if you were to direct the forensics program at that school.

NOTES

1. Chapter 1 discusses the rationale for forensics participation. See also Marjorie Keeshan Nadler, "The Gender Factor in Selecting Extra-Curricular Activities." *National Forensic Journal*, 3 (1985): 29–36.
2. Cf. Michael Roloff, *Interpersonal Communication: The Social Exchange Approach*. (Beverly Hills: Sage, 1981).
3. Charles R. Berger, "Task Performance and Attributional Communication as Determinants of Interpersonal Attraction." *Speech Monographs*, 40 (1973): 280–286.
4. See also Kevin W. Dean and Kenda Creasy Dean, "Forensic Recruiting Within the University." *National Forensic Journal*, 3 (1985): 37–54. This article also contains some very useful examples of recruiting tools that could be adapted for use in high schools.
5. Douglas McGregor, *The Human Side of Enterprise*. (New York: McGraw-Hill, 1960). A similar and more recent analysis is supplied by R. E. Lester, "Organizational Culture, Uncertainty Reduction, and the Socialization of New Organizational Members." In S. Thomas, ed., *Studies in Communication: Culture and Communication*. vol. 3. (Norwood: Ablex, 1987).
6. Paul Watzlawick, Janet Beavin, and Don Jackson, *The Pragmatics of Human Communication*. (New York: W. W. Norton, 1967).
7. Thomas Peters and Robert Waterman, *In Search of Excellence: Lessons from America's Best-Run Companies*. (New York: Harper & Row, 1982).
8. Raymond Ross, *Small Groups in Organizational Settings*. (Englewood Cliffs: Prentice Hall, 1989). Chapter 1.
9. A Zero-Sum game refers to the fact that there will be one winner and one loser.
10. Sharon B. Porter and Michael Sommerness, "Legal Issues Confronting the Director of Forensics." *National Forensic Journal*, 9 (1991): 109–123.

APPENDIX TO CHAPTER 4

Public Relations Activities

The following appendix gives further information on public relations activities. It provides basic information on how to create press releases, along with some examples. This information is excerpted from *Media Resource Guide*, (1987), edited by David McElwee, Foundation for American Communications, pp. 11–15.

RELEASING INFORMATION

You can write a news release and mail it to reporters and editors. You can hand deliver it. You can include a background package. You can include photographs. These are just a few of the decisions to be made when releasing information.

The first step in releasing information is evaluation. Is the information news? What is the most interesting part of your information as a news story? What is the best and most appropriate place to seek time or space?

Besides newsworthiness you must also evaluate your information in terms of its most logical and effective media targets.

After determining your targets, the next step is to form and shape your information into news stories for the various news outlets you have targeted. This may involve shaping different stories from the same information for different news organizations. . . .

You have to view the story through the eyes of the news organization's reporter and editor to determine the best way to sell it.

This is not an easy task. If it were easy, there would not be nearly 800 listings for public relations and publicity services in the Manhattan phone book, or nearly 600 in Los Angeles, or more than 200 in Washington, D. C.

But even professional publicists generally restrict themselves to a handful for proven effective methods for releasing information. The most common is the news release, an instrument that is central to any good media relations program. It is so important that it deserves special attention. . . . Other key vehicles for releasing information include press conferences and interviews. . . .

When should the information be released? While each story will have its own characteristics, you should be sensitive to the deadlines of the media as well as your own time frame.

NEWS RELEASES

The newsrooms of America are in constant danger of being buried in a paper blizzard of news releases. Because of their volume, not all news releases are carefully read, thoughtfully considered, or thoroughly evaluated for news content. Whoever reads your news release will be someone in a hurry. That person must be able to tell at a glance if there is any hope of finding something newsworthy. Any idea you present must jump off the page, if your news release is to survive the first screening.

If possible, provide a short summary or news memo covering the major points of your story. This helps the editor find the news more quickly and improves the chances of your release being covered.

If your story is complicated, add background information. This additional material may take different forms: a scientific study, perhaps, or a chronological history of past developments in the story — if it is a new angle of a long-running story.

Generally, news releases should be as short as possible while containing all the important facts. . . .

Public relations professionals consider the news release worthy of special effort. Every effort should be made to write it in journalistic style. Then compare your writing with news stories in your target news outlets.

Material written this way is easier for the busy reporter or editor to absorb quickly and easily.

Most reporters and editors will consider your news release the starting point of a story. On the other hand, don't be surprised when an especially well-written news release is used word for word. In newswriting, the vital elements of a story are given quickly and concisely. The first paragraph usually tells the reader all major facts by answering six critical questions: Who? What? When? Where? Why? and How?

Newswriting follows the "inverted pyramid" style in which every paragraph is considered more important than the ones following it.

This bears repeating: in news style, the story is written in descending order of importance. This means getting the news up front. A busy reader who is not interested by the first paragraph will not read the second one.

Newswriting is stark compared to scholarly efforts. Sentences and paragraphs should be short. Everyday words must be used. Please translate "solid state barrier control" to the more widely used "doorknob."

Avoid jargon and technical terms. You don't have to go overboard and translate words into primary school vocabulary. Just remember you are more knowledgeable, specifically trained, or at least have more exposure to the topic than the newsperson and the public.

There are limitations on news releases. A news release sent to many potential users is "nonexclusive." You'll learn quickly how important some information can be if it is "exclusive." On top of that, a mass-produced and distributed news release will generally be too shallow for some potential users—and too deep for others.

Another limitation is the commonness of news releases. So many releases are issued every day by so many sources that the media gatekeepers will scan rather than scrutinize these offerings.

While the limitations are real, they should not negate the value of a news release. Remember, too, that you, as the source of the information, have a great deal of control over the information. For instance, you determine the time of its release. In most cases, your news should be for "immediate release." If you are timing your release to an event, you can designate the date and time of the event as the time when the information is "released" for use. Be careful, though, the attitude of many editors is that if a piece of information is news, it is news today or whenever they want to print or broadcast it.

Generally, the source also controls who releases the information, what information is released, where it is released and why and how it is released.

Finally, make sure that you, as the source, are clearly identified on the news release along with addresses and phone numbers where you can be reached. The idea is to make it easy for a writer or editor to reach you if he or she has questions about your release. Use your letterhead on the first page. If you find that you are sending out many releases, you might want to have news release forms printed.

Sample News Release

Contact: Dean Swartz
FAX: 213/851-7372

LOS ANGELES - Basic guidelines for writing and sending out successful news releases were suggested today at a News Media Relations Workshop by Dean Swartz, director of communications, Foundation for American Communications.

News releases should be cleanly typed or copied on 8 1/2 by 11 inch paper, Swartz said. They should be hand-delivered or mailed First Class to the designated target media, including radio and television stations, weekly and daily newspapers, and appropriate magazines. Wire services should not be overlooked, he said.

Other guidelines are:

IDENTIFICATION: The sending organization should be identified plainly. Use your letterhead or printed news release forms. The name and telephone number of a contact for additional information must appear at the top of the page.

RELEASE DATE: Most releases should be "immediate" or "for use upon receipt." Stipulate a release time only when there is a specific reason such as a speech, a news announcement, or a meeting involved in the news being released.

MARGINS: Leave wide margins and space at the top, so the editors can edit.

HEADLINES: If you want to use a headline, remember it's just to summarize your writing, not something they will use.

LENGTH: Never use more than one page unless you must; never more than two pages. If you have a long release, get all the highlights into a terse memo and attach the information to it as background material.

STYLE: Use the summary lead and five w's (who, what, when, where, why, and sometimes, how) most of the time. Double space. Short sentences and active verbs are better than others. Edit material tightly. Make sure it's accurate, timely, and not blatantly self-serving. Don't split a paragraph from the first to second page. Put "more" at the bottom of the first page.

AVOID: Fancy, stilted wording. Translate into plain English language. Don't shout NEWS or hype your news release.

CHECK: Double check names, spellings, numbers, grammar. Proofread carefully.

PLACEMENT: Your news release should be in the hands of the editors at least 24 hours before any event or activity you are publicizing. You should know in advance to whom to deliver your news releases. General news goes to the city desk or assignment editor. Specialized news should be given directly to reporters or departments, especially if they know you or vice versa.

AT END: Put "30" or "###"

Sample News Memo

To:	Addressed to editor or reporter
From:	You
Re:	A one- or two-sentence statement regarding the story you are suggesting, the event to which you are inviting the reporters, or other purpose of the news release.
Time & Date:	Specific time, date, year.
Location:	Specific location, including directions if the location is off the beaten path.
Why:	You must have a reason for the news release or the event. You will be more successful if you can say why and provide enough information for the decision maker to decide to accept your invitation for coverage.
Contact:	The name and phone number of someone the news editor or reporter can contact with questions about your news release.

Part II
FORENSICS AS
TEACHING AND LEARNING

Part I of this text analyzes forensics as a system, laying out the structure of the activity as organizational, educational, and interpersonal systems. Part II shifts gears from general systems analysis into a discussion of forensics as "teaching and learning" systems. If Part I describes "what" forensics is, Part II describes "how" it is done and, more important, how to teach and learn it.

The chapters in Part II cover the educational domain of the program, including the subsystems of teaching/coaching and teaching/judging. They examine teaching individual events, teaching debate, and teaching through judging competitive forensics events. These are three principal contexts for teaching and learning in forensics. There are, of course, other forensics events, such as Reader's Theatre and Student Congress. These are more specialized and sound resources available to guide their teaching.[1] While it is dangerous to describe the "typical" forensics program, the usual prototype is a program that competes in either individual events and debate or both and attends competitive tournaments. This is the assumption that guides the choice of materials in the next three chapters.

It should be noted that another model, in which forensics is solely an intramural activity, also is occasionally used by schools. Using this model, a school might substitute on-campus and in-class activities for competition with other schools. This model is followed in circumstances where geographic distances or inadequate financial resources prevent a school from using the competitive model. While many of the concepts in the following chapters are specifically targeted toward use of the competitive model, they also are useful, through modification, for the intramural model.

Part II concludes with chapters containing learning resources and ethical issues pertaining to forensics.

5
Teaching Individual Events

CHAPTER OVERVIEW

This chapter discusses teaching individual events. It begins with an overview of the educational domain and the role of individual events in forensics education. A philosophy of individual events, based on rhetorical principles, is then introduced. The chapter defines commonly used speaking events and concludes by providing some suggestions for teaching individual events.

THE EDUCATIONAL DOMAIN

As introduced in Chapter 4, a domain is an area of emphasis within a system. The chapter looked at interpersonal and organizational domains of a program. This chapter takes a close look at educational practices, examining these practices using the rhetorical perspective. This perspective considers forensics, as you recall, as a form of rhetorical scholarship where speakers create messages and adapt them to their audiences.

This chapter discusses teaching and learning individual events. The first section will discuss the learning philosophy of individual events as forensics. The second section will describe commonly used events. The third section will introduce a teaching strategy, grounded in rhetorical theory, for helping students prepare for competition.

Before going further an important caveat is necessary. The practice of individual events is rapidly changing. Creation of national collegiate championships in individual events has encouraged increasing innovation and change in individual events practice. These changes find their way to other college and high school programs. Competitive success depends, in part, on understanding current trends in practice. This will be found by observing other competitors and staying current with the literature in the area.

THE PHILOSOPHY OF INDIVIDUAL EVENTS

Public speaking instruction dates back to antiquity. Teachers justified its instruction initially because they believed it was a valuable citizenship tool. Rhetorical scholars and teachers developed different philosophies to guide their instruction. These scholars did not see public speaking solely as a tool, but as part of a holistic education. Current teaching of individual events shares this aim. This section discusses the philosophical assumptions guiding the teaching of individual events. In discussing individual events from a philosophical perspective, the discussion must be subdivided. We will examine the justification for individual events, the philosophy of teaching the events, and the role of competition in the process.

The Educational Values of Individual Events

There are four educational benefits that students may gain through competing in individual events. First, individual events competition ought to teach good public speaking skills. Second, it ought to teach sound analysis and reasoning skills. Third, it ought to build courage. Fourth, it ought to increase aesthetic appreciation of language. This list is not hierarchical. Different events emphasize these values differently. Oral interpretation events, for example, probably are stronger at building aesthetic appreciation than extemporaneous speaking. Extemporaneous speaking, on the other hand, places greater emphasis on analysis and reasoning. Each individual event, however, can only be justified because it contributes to building these skills.

Public Speaking Skills

The most common reason justifying individual events is their role in building public speaking skills. Selecting a topic or interpretation selection, writing, and then delivering a speech teaches very useful skills. These skills are transferable to endless contexts where people value public speaking. Employers, for instance, prize oral communication skills highly in making hiring and promotion choices.

Analytical Skills

The second justification is the role of individual events in building analysis and reasoning skills. Students may benefit from the process of "invention" where the speaker selects an appropriate topic and arguments based on her analysis of the audience and context. The belief that such skills can be learned underlies the rationale for the study of rhetoric since classical times. Contemporary public speaking and persuasion pedagogy emphasizes the importance of audience analysis and adaptation as central to the act of public speaking.[2]

Similarly, participating in oral interpretation events can build student skill in literary analysis. While competitors often are not required to develop a theme in their performance they still must analyze their material to select appropriate excerpts to present in the competitive round. They must analyze the material to understand the author's meaning and the mood and logic of the piece they will present.

The variety of audiences in forensics competition may be helpful in encouraging good analysis and adaptation skills. Furthermore, the relative sophistication of the audience as trained listeners may encourage the use of sound analysis and reasoning. This is true since the audience presumably would not be influenced by specious reasons, such as the ones commonly associated with advertisements.

The fact that audiences are occasionally influenced by specious reasons makes it very important for speakers to develop a sound ethical grounding for their speeches. Speakers must learn, as discussed in Chapter 9, the need for creating "good reasons."

Personal Growth

The third educational rationale is the role of individual events in building courage and enhancing personal growth. Public speaking causes anxiety for many people. While this anxiety usually is mild, the number of situations requiring public speaking doubtless exacerbates the anxiety. While not a universal cure for anxiety, practice in writing and delivering speeches is helpful in "demystifying" the public speaking act. Getting up and speaking addresses some underlying fears that the speaker will appear foolish to the audience. The student may fear blanking out during the speech or fear he will use some embarrassing word or gesture.

Language Appreciation

The fourth rationale for individual events is increasing aesthetic appreciation for language. Public speaking is, in a sense, as much an art form as music and theater. Oral interpretation, in fact, is often seen as an adjunct to the study of theater. Ancient Greeks considered public speaking an integral part of their culture, and used epideictic speeches as means of celebrating important occasions.

Many famous speeches blur the distinction between speech and art. The Gettysburg Address, MacArthur's Farewell Address, and King's Lincoln Memorial speech are three notable examples. We consider these speeches not only as communicative events but as artifacts appreciated for their beauty and permanence. These speakers elevate the speech beyond the occasion to something that has universal significance and appeal.

Individual events competition ought to enhance our understanding of the aesthetic elements of speech and language. Oral interpretation, for example, is an opportunity for students to better appreciate literature. Writing, presenting, and listening to speeches ought to encourage students' appreciation of the difficulty involved in writing a "good" speech.

These goals will be returned to when discussing teaching strategies later in this chapter. At this point turn to the second aspect of our philosophy discussion, the role of the teacher in individual events.

The Philosophy of Teaching Individual Events

For new forensics teachers with background in communication and public speaking, individual events instruction will be distinctly similar to regular public speaking instruction. You will discover some particular unique nuances of competitive speaking, but the basic ideas and skills will be the same. There are several aspects of a teaching philosophy for individual events worthy of mention.

1. *Students should take primary responsibility for the invention process.* Individual events should not be like sports where the coach calls the plays. Students should be responsible for selecting a topic and preparing and polishing the speech or interpretation selection.

The teacher should, however, be active in each step of the process. The role of the teacher is to set goals, help resolve problems, and react to creation of the product. The teacher, for instance, could say, "Your topic is weak," but should not give the student a topic, or write all or even parts of the speech.

Some people occasionally argue that teachers can model good speeches through active involvement in the invention process. This justification lacks merit. Achieving the educational benefits we just discussed requires that the student "get their hands dirty" by engaging in the invention process, even if they occasionally fail. Failure is, of course, often as valuable as success in creating real learning. Failure helps the student generalize the skills he is learning to many contexts through learning why he was unsuccessful in a particular case. If teachers remove the risk of failure, they limit the chances for long-term, worthwhile learning.

You should not, of course, interpret this to mean that all failures are useful. The role of the teacher must be to help the student learn from those experiences and internalize the lesson, so that frustration does not set in.

For example, the teacher must help the student understand "why" his topic was unsuccessful, so the student does not go out and pick another unsuccessful topic.

2. *The teacher should articulate universal goals rather than short-term goals.* The teacher ought to set out a clear educational philosophy for the students emphasizing the long-term benefits of individual events competition. This involves explanation of process issues. The teacher must explain "why" a speech is written in a particular way, or why audience analysis is important. Individual events competition is most educationally significant when students internalize the process instead of focusing on the immediate product.

This can be a difficult task. It is human nature to be caught up in the present. The student may be primarily concerned with the "end" of a winning speech or selection, and uninterested in the "means" of getting there. Furthermore, since we can reduce public speaking to a series of "formulas" (first you pick a topic, then you research the topic, and so on), it becomes easier to teach the formula than its underlying rationale.

A certain amount of forensics teaching must, therefore, involve formal discussion of process issues and not just individualized instruction where the steps in the public speaking formula are checked-off after completion.

3. *Students should have broad preparation by participating in multiple events.* The final philosophical concern here is the question of specialization versus broad preparation. Should students become "expert" by concentrating on learning a single event, or should they prepare for many different events? Should they trade off breadth in knowledge for skill in a particular event? These are difficult questions. While there are excellent reasons justifying either approach, the stronger case can be made for broad preparation.

Specialization does have its justifications. It may create competitive success, greater understanding of the content of a speech, and compensate for time pressures from other activities. The student probably will be more competitively successful since they will devote more time to improving their presentation in their event. The student also will become more expert in the content area of her presentation. As we discussed earlier, some programs depend heavily on winning as their measure of success. In other situations, competing demands on student time (such as classes or jobs) may dictate that a student specializes to receive any benefits from forensics. This case for specialization may be contrasted with the one for broad preparation.

There are several benefits of broad preparation. The most important is that no single individual event can deliver all the educational benefits that can be derived from forensics competition. Experience in more events expands the repertoire of skills the student can apply in other contexts.

Participating in several events also creates a greater sense of perspective for the student. This should allow them to appreciate the breadth of the activity and the people participating in it.

Another benefit of broad participation, especially for beginning students, is that it gives them the ability to pick the events they may want to specialize in or perhaps study further. A student may, for instance, have a negative impression of oral interpretation. Participating in that event could inspire a previously unknown interest or aptitude.

By way of anticipation of our discussion of debate, the principle of broad participation also extends to participating in both debate and individual events. Neither debate nor individual events by themselves create the holistic benefits of forensics training. In fact, there has been a trend in recent years for programs to specialize in either debate or individual events. This trend is explained by citing scarce resources as reasons for specialization. A more realistic and honest explanation, however, is simply the competitive imperative. Programs sometimes are more successful in winning awards if they concentrate their preparation on a few events. In this situation, programs emphasizing only debate or individual events for students place convenience or competitive success above the greater need for more complete student education.

The Philosophy of Competition in Individual Events

The final philosophical issue is the role of competition in teaching individual events. As noted earlier, competitive individual events have particular nuances that differentiate these events from classroom or real-world speaking. These nuances are a product of attempting to create competitive success, and are examined in the next section. But the philosophical issues are highlighted here, of which there are several emerging from competition in individual events.

1. *Competition, by itself, is insufficient training in public speaking.* Forensic competition is not, nor does it claim to be, a perfect mirror of the real world. Tournaments characteristically have small or even nonexistent audiences sharing more similarities than differences. The types of events and their rules hopefully encourage both competition and education. These rules do not, however, correspond precisely to the kind of speaking people do in other contexts. While forensic training is useful, it is only a part of a complete education.

Students receive a more complete education when they have both competitive and noncompetitive opportunities. Schools must expose students to a wide range of speaking contexts with a variety of audiences and occasions for speaking. Speakers must face the challenge of adapting their competitive speeches to new audiences. For example, speakers should have the chance to present their speech to public groups, such as service organizations. These audiences do not care whether a speech conforms to competitive rules, but listen for the content of the speech.

This noncompetitive speaking encourages the student to internalize the speaking process and go beyond the immediacy of creating a speech only for presentation in a competitive environment. A program need not sacrifice its competitive focus for noncompetitive speaking activities. Such events may not require much time or money. There are countless places where students can give speeches in the community or on campus. Maximizing these opportunities is also a valuable public relations tool.

2. *High ethical standards are important.* The text looks at ethical issues in the last chapter, but emphasizes the philosophical perspective here. Unfortunately, forensics competition creates an environment where unethical practices can achieve competitive success.

Creating good speeches or finding good oral interpretation selections is difficult. The student may not find all the research material they need to complete their speech. A play written for performance on stage may not easily fit the requirements of an interpretation contest. The student, having invested energy in preparing the speech or interpretation selection, may want it to be successful despite preparation problems. Sometimes the speaker will be tempted to create an imaginary statistic that will "punch up" the speech, or rearrange a story or play to make its presentation easier.

The structure of the activity makes it likely that abuses will be undetected in the short term. Competitors generally are not required to submit manuscripts and the listener rarely will be as familiar with the speaking material as the speaker. These conditions make high ethical behaviors by competitors even more critical. Therefore, clear program guidelines on ethics are important to encouraging ethical behavior. Forensics teachers must constantly verbalize the need for high ethics and their unwillingness to tolerate unethical behavior.

3. *Good listening is important.* Individual events competitors will spend much more time listening than speaking, even if they compete in multiple events. Some tournaments allow students to leave after presenting their speech or do not require the competitor to listen to other speakers. This is both philosophically and pragmatically undesirable.

From a philosophical perspective, students learn by listening. They gain much understanding by watching others succeed or fail. Furthermore, good listening is intrinsic to effective communication. Forensics competition provides a useful method of learning good listening skills. Listening is a communication skill that almost everyone needs to improve, and is also crucial to real-world success.

In addition, there is pragmatic justification for encouraging students to listen to other speakers. Doing so gives them insight into the kinds of strategies that are successful and unsuccessful. They can place their presentation in perspective with those of other competitors. Having an audience also helps other speakers to be successful. Assuming the audience behaves politely and supportively, a larger audience can help build the confidence of other speakers, enhancing the activity. Finally, listening to others, and having a supportive audience, builds the confidence of the speaker. They see others with the same kinds of fears. They also benefit from seeing friendly faces to reinforce their confidence.

In summary, this section attempts to articulate some philosophical issues connected with teaching and learning individual events. The section discusses the educational values of individual events, pedagogical questions, and issues connected to the role of competition. The next section discusses the types of individual events and their characteristics.

TYPES OF INDIVIDUAL EVENTS

Individual events can be divided into categories. The two primary categories are *public address* events and *oral interpretation* events. Each of these general categories can be further subdivided, as is seen in Figure 5.1.

FIGURE 5.1 Categorization of individual events.

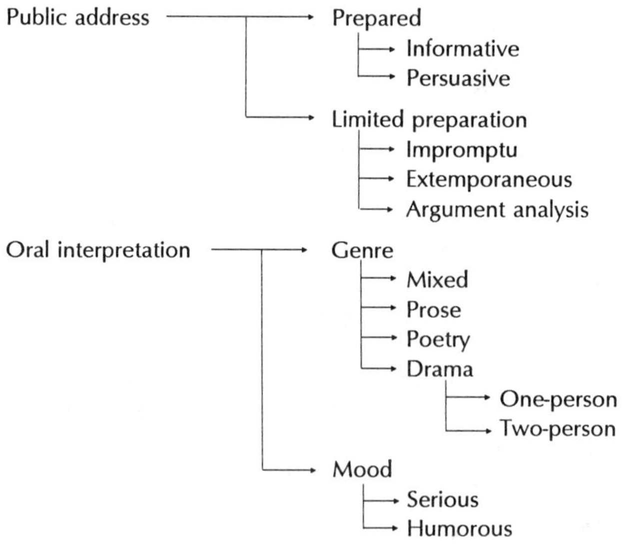

Public address includes events where the speaker prepares and delivers an original speech. Prepared speeches call for the speaker writing the speech before the tournament on a topic of his choice. The speech may either have a general purpose of informing or persuading the audience. Limited preparation events give the speaker only a short time at the tournament to create a speech on a topic given to him. These speeches can be informative or persuasive in nature.

In oral interpretation events the speaker interprets a written work of an author other than herself. We categorize these events either by genre or mood. Genres include prose, poetry, and so on. Moods are either serious or humorous selections and can be drawn from any genre. The kinds of events usually included in individual events competition match the category.

Prepared Public Address Events

These events represent the kinds of speeches most commonly associated with public speaking activity. Sometimes people call these speeches "platform" speaking, alluding to standing on a platform to present the speech.

Prepared public address events can be categorized by their speech purpose — either informative or persuasive — as seen in Figure 5.2.

Speeches with an informative purpose intend to present the audience with new information about an object, idea, or process. Persuasive speeches intend to either reinforce or change the beliefs, values, or actions of the audience. The distinctions between these two purposes are artificial and often illusory. The distinctions only serve to guide the speaker's organization and language choices and to guide the judge in evaluating the speech in competition.

Expository speeches (sometimes called *informative speeches*) describe or explain an idea, object, or process. The topic should have some potential significance and relevance to the audience. The main characteristic of informative speeches is the common use of audio or visual aids for helping the audience understand the subject. Time limits for the speech are seven to ten minutes, and the speech may be memorized. Both high schools and college tournaments commonly use this event.

FIGURE 5.2   Prepared public address events.

INFORMATIVE	PERSUASIVE
Expository	Persuasive (oratory)
Communication analysis	Editorial commentary
Rhetorical criticism	Radio speaking
	Sales
	After dinner speaking

Communication analysis and *rhetorical criticism* are variations on a single idea, the analysis of public discourse through application of a model to an artifact or event. A model can be either a theory or analytic tool that the speaker can apply to some speech or other communication event to help the audience better understand both the event and the model applied to the event. The general purpose of each speech is to provide the audience with greater insight into the artifact (a speech or a commercial) or event (a political campaign or the Persian Gulf War). While organized like an informative speech, these speeches have two distinct parts—selection of a model and application of the model to the artifact or event. The speaker usually selects a model from ones used by communication scholars.

The study of rhetorical criticism has been a dominant form of communication study since the beginning of the twentieth century. The study has grown rapidly in recent years through addition of various analytic tools. There are excellent textbooks available to introduce the student to the process of rhetorical criticism and the various models available.[3] Some commonly used models include those listed in Figure 5.3

This is literally only the tip of the iceberg. There are probably hundreds of potential models that could appropriately be used. In fact, choice of a "new" model may often help the speech stand out from others. This event is found primarily in college competition. The usual time limits are eight to ten minutes. The speech may be memorized or delivered from manuscript and often includes visual aids.

Persuasive speaking (sometimes called *oratory*) is possibly the oldest form of platform speaking. As discussed in an earlier chapter, the study of persuasion is ancient, dating back to classical Greece. Important throughout the history of Western civilization, persuasive speaking is an integral part of life in the United States. Inaugural addresses, political stump speeches, and impassioned addresses to juries are just several examples of the important role of persuasive speaking skills in public affairs. There are persuasive speaking contests in many places outside forensics competition. Many schools and civic organizations sponsor persuasive speaking contests, often on topics germane to the interests of the organization. Examples of

FIGURE 5.3   Some potential models for communication analysis and rhetorical criticism speeches.

> Aristotelian Model of Persuasion
> Stephen Toulmin's Model of Argument
> Kenneth Burke's Dramatism
> Walter Fisher's Theory of Narrative
> Feminist criticism
> Fantasy theme analysis
> The classical idea of *apologia*

these contests include ones sponsored by The Veterans of Foreign Wars, Toastmasters, and Optimists Clubs, among others.

Persuasive speeches attempt to change or reinforce the beliefs, values, or actions of the audience. There are two general types of persuasive speeches—*pragmatic* and *philosophical*. Pragmatic persuasive speeches are action oriented, specifying the particular actions the speaker wishes the audience to take. Philosophical persuasive speeches are less specific, attempting to influence the beliefs and values of the listener.[4]

Persuasive speeches typically are eight to ten minutes in length and often are memorized. While rules often do not prohibit the use of audio or visual aids, they are less often used in persuasive speaking than informative speeches.

Editorial commentary and *radio speaking* are variations on the same idea. In each case the purpose of the speech is to emulate a television or radio commentator making a brief presentation of an editorial position.

The topics of these speeches typically are grounded in current events and may or may not include a specific proposed action. The principal defining characteristic of the speeches is their length. Rules often precisely limit the speech to a period such as 1.45 to 2 minutes, emulating the length of television or radio editorial presentations.

Sales speaking is another type of persuasive speech where the speaker attempts to "sell" a product to the audience. The speaker often uses visual aids or the actual product as part of the persuasive presentation.

After dinner speeches attempt to make a serious point by using humor. The term *after dinner speaking* refers to the tradition of banquet speaking dating back as far as the nineteenth century, when audiences prized speakers who could effectively use humor in their speeches to entertain.

As a contemporary forensic event, after dinner speaking may more closely resemble a Johnny Carson or Bob Hope monologue than a nineteenth-century banquet address. There is greater emphasis on the humorous than the serious elements of the speech. The speech is organized similarly to other speeches, is usually memorized, and often uses visual aids. The after dinner speech may combine elements of both persuasive and informative speaking. This same comment is probably true of most forensics speeches.

There are, at best, subtle differences between informative and persuasive speeches. A speaker could potentially develop any topic in either way. The difference would come in the organization and writing of the speech.

First, informative and persuasive speeches often use language differently. Persuasive language is often more value-laden and language techniques are chosen for their ability to motivate action. A sermon, for example, uses very different language than a corporate briefing.

Second, the speeches typically use different organizational patterns. Since the purpose of informative speeches is to describe or explain, these speeches often use organizational patterns such as "structure and function" or "topical" organization, emphasizing acquiring new information. Persuasive speeches normally include motivational and action elements designed to influence behavior.

The decision to treat a topic as an informative or persuasive event depends mostly on the interests of the student and her understanding of the topic.

Limited Preparation Public Address

The second major type of individual events are the limited preparation public address events. These events may either use a persuasive or informative focus. The main difference from prepared events is in teaching students to prepare speeches in a short period. Students learn to speak "on their feet" or "off the cuff."

There are various practical applications for this skill. People may confront situations, at business or civic meetings for example, when they have the opportunity to speak although they did not prepare a speech in advance. Mastery of speech preparation skills also helps students confidently and actively to participate in the substantial number of social and political contexts involving public speaking.

Limited participation does not imply a lack of any preparation although one event, impromptu speaking, seems to imply as much. Successful contestants in these events do considerable preparation and anticipate the expectations posed by each event.

Extemporaneous speaking is a limited preparation event during which the speaker is given a choice of three topics and allowed a half hour to write a speech. The topics are typically in the area of current events and the speech time is usually six or seven minutes. Sometimes the judge asks the speaker a question at the conclusion of the speech.

Impromptu speaking differs in the sense that the speaker draws a topic and speaks almost immediately. In accordance, impromptu speaking topics are sometimes broader and more philosophical than extemporaneous topics. It is typical, for example, for contests to use quotations or single words as topics. The speaker might present a speech on a topic such as: "Friendship" or "Winning Isn't Everything, It's the Only Thing."

Speakers prepare for both these events by reading books and magazines in current events and philosophy. Speakers typically save articles in files that may help them write a speech, particularly for extemporaneous speaking. Speakers also familiarize themselves with organizational patterns that they can use, and do considerable practicing.[5]

Argument analysis is an event where the speaker draws a topic using an artifact (such as an editorial or advertisement) and has limited time to prepare a speech analyzing the arguments presented in the artifact.

Once again, there are two types of public speaking events — prepared and unprepared events. These speeches are either persuasive or informative in purpose. The second major category of individual events is oral interpretation events.

Oral Interpretation

Oral interpretation is the term classifying the events grouped together as the second individual event type. The oral interpretation discipline traces its roots back to classical Greece. For many centuries, story tellers (such as the mythical Homer) were not only entertainment, but crucial to transmitting knowledge and culture.[6] Bridging both the study of rhetoric and drama, oral interpretation today is valuable both for improving communication skills and strengthening aesthetic appreciation of literature.

Oral interpretation has been a contest event since the beginning of competitive contest speaking. Until recent times its use was almost exclusively limited to programmed reading. In this event, a student interpreted several literary excerpts from one or more genres, selected to develop a central theme. Consistent with the rapid growth of individual events competition since 1970, oral interpretation events have literally exploded in number and popularity.

Oral interpretation events are divided by either genre or mood, and by the number of people participating in the presentation (see Figure 5.1, p. 82). The genre events include: prose, poetry, and drama interpretation. In each case, the contestant selects one or more selections attempting to illustrate a theme. Many tournaments still have programmed reading contests where contestants interpret several selections from a mixture of genres. Another common method is to divide events by the mood the literature illustrates, either humorous or serious. Finally, an increasingly popular event is two-person (duo) interpretation where two people interpret two or more play characters.

Whatever type, the format and characteristics of oral interpretation contests are generally the same. First, interpretation selections must "give the illusion of reading." Oral interpretation differs from theater in that interpreters do not memorize their lines and "become" the characters. They instead attempt to convey to the audience the "meaning" of the author's words. Use of a script discourages the same suspension of disbelief found in the theater.[7]

Second, interpretation selections are chosen to illustrate a theme. Judges critique interpretation presentations not only on the skill of the interpreter but on the success of the interpreter of relating the selection to a particular theme. The theme may either be specific or general. The theme is the analytical tool the speaker uses to provide a context for his interpretation.

Third, the quality of literature is an important aspect of the oral interpretation contest. Since one justification for oral interpretation is in increasing a student's aesthetic appreciation skills, students are either implicitly or explicitly judged on the quality of the literature they interpret.

There is disagreement about the importance of evaluating the quality of literature and these other traditional oral interpretation elements. There is a recent trend toward moving oral interpretation away from its traditional grounding and aligning its study more closely to theater. This performance studies movement, when applied to oral interpretation contests, would allow interpreters more freedom to discard the illusion of reading, deemphasize use of themes, and allow use of literary forms that are not traditionally used. Changing attitudes about oral interpretation reflect, of course, a dynamic and changing system adapting to disciplinary changes in the oral interpretation discipline. The performance studies perspective is gradually gaining strength in forensics, particularly at the college level.[8]

The Unique Characteristics of Individual Events

We began this section by hinting at particular nuances of individual events that make these speeches different from other speaking contexts. We return to this subject for two reasons. First, these characteristics help to describe the events and second, they also point to the kinds of teaching strategies appropriate for preparing students to compete in the events. Preparing students for competition is the subject of the final section of this chapter.

Individual events prepare students for a wide variety of public speaking contests. However, the *performance* of the events in competition may be different from how a person might perform a speech in other speaking situations. This is similar to the differences between professional and schoolyard sports. Baseball consists of throwing, hitting, and catching a ball. But a game in very different in a city park than in Yankee Stadium! Perhaps in an ideal world, there would not be substantial differences between contest speaking and other forms. Obviously, the greatest transference of skills is achieved when students use contest speaking to build the exact skills they will need in other contexts. There are, however, some unique nuances of competitive speaking events that make those speeches different from other situations.

1. *Audiences are small or nonexistent.* The structure of tournaments limits the use of audiences for the speaking contests. The need to justify the large expense of forensics dictates that students compete in multiple rounds, and often in multiple events. This makes it less likely that any given round, other than an occasional final round, will have more than one judge and a few other contestants. In addition, the typical judge is a person with some training in forensics or public speaking. She may be looking at different factors in the speech than would an audience listening for other purposes.

2. *Feedback is delayed.* The tournament structure generally does not give time for the speaker and judge to interact after the speech. Usually, the speaker's primary feedback comes from the written ballot, submitted after the tournament. This is an inefficient system in the sense that it is more difficult to understand written comments about a speech given earlier, and the speaker does not have a chance to seek clarification from the judge about the comments.

Different judges also will have different and sometimes contradictory comments about a speaker or speech. This also can be confusing for a speaker when sorting out conflicting advice.

3. *Individual events competition is rule bound.* Contest speaking is unique in that there is a high dependence on following particular competitive rules. Speech time-limits, for instance, are strictly enforced. Speakers speaking longer than the maximum usually are penalized. Other rules may specify such things as the number of quoted words or types of visual aids that can be used. This means that judges are more likely to critique speakers on how well they follow the rules than on their overall speaking abilities.

One important rule is the use of particular event descriptions, such as informative or persuasive speaking. This is different from speaking in other contexts, where the speaker may combine persuasive and informative elements in a speech. The speaker might even face a context where they may choose the purpose for the speech.

4. *Competitors often use a competitive style.* Competitive speakers are often more polished speakers, and may use particular speaking techniques designed to fit the particular speaking situation. An extemporaneous speaking competitor, for example, may use an organizational pattern with three major sections, no matter whether another pattern may be more appropriate. The speaker does this to fit with the expectations of the judges. As a competitive system, forensics is characterized by particular situational expectations about what "good" speaking and speakers are. This sometimes leads to speaking styles that are different from styles appropriate for other contexts.

These differences all stem from forensics as a competitive system. None of these nuances creates a particular problem or liability for the student. The student can master the situational constraints on speaking easily, and then generalize the more important skills when they leave competition. The final section of this chapter concerns teaching and learning strategies for mastering both the situational elements of competitive speaking and the underlying public speaking skills.

TEACHING AND LEARNING STRATEGIES FOR INDIVIDUAL EVENTS COMPETITION

There is no secret formula for teaching and learning individual events. The sheer number of events, differences in event rules and competitive practices in various regions, and the dynamic nature of the forensic activity make generalizations about learning strategies unproductive. Changing conditions also will alter what can be considered good teaching strategies, so successful forensics teaching requires a teacher to do three things: (1) Develop a sound basic educational philosophy and set of teaching strategies; (2) Be flexible and able to adapt their strategies to new conditions; and (3) Allow students to take primary responsibility for their own learning.

The purpose of this book obviously is to help the teacher develop an educational philosophy for teaching forensics. The purpose of this section is to suggest a pedagogical framework for teaching individual events using rhetorical principles. The teacher can use this rhetorical framework, the learning resources documented elsewhere in this book (especially Chapter 8), the large number of public speaking and oral interpretation textbooks, common sense, and observation of other successful teachers to devise teaching strategies appropriate for their particular forensics program.

Creating a teaching strategy for learning public speaking skills is, of course, not a new challenge. Some early teachers, the Sophists, attempted to teach rhetorical forms for persuasion without teaching content or truth. This approach was later discredited, and now we use *sophistry* as an insult for artful speech without content. In the nineteenth century, elocutionists attempted to teach speech skills through rote memorization of speaking techniques and gestures based on a model of "great speakers." Even contemporary public relations experts caution their clients to follow the script by dressing, speaking, and behaving in ways calculated to best appeal to the television eye.

These strategies all assume that public speaking can be taught by breaking the act down into its smallest parts and having the student master each of those parts. The teacher attempts to create success formulas to minimize the chances for competitive or learning failures.

Another approach, and the one advocated in this text, views teaching of public speaking from a more holistic perspective. It views a speech as a system, analogous to the organizational scheme of this text, which views forensics from a systems perspective. Each speech is unique in the sense that the speaker will emphasize the speech components in a different way for each speech. The systems principle of "equifinality" suggests that there are many ways that a speech can be effectively written and presented.

This philosophy is not new, but one introduced centuries ago in the classical work, the *Rhetorica Ad Herennium*. The author of this important work is unknown, but the teaching system for speaking it introduces — rhetorical "canons" or principles — greatly influenced rhetoricians from Roman times until the present.[9] Figure 5.4 diagrams, in its broadest sense, the theory of rhetorical canons.

The canons are the various parts of the speaking process combined together to create the finished product. Each canon is both a system and a subsystem of the speech. The speaker must master all the canons to create a finished product. The competent speaker understands and applies the principles of each canon to create the successful speech.

Invention is the process of selecting a topic. This process involves analyzing the occasion and audience to find a topic that will fit the occasion and interest the audience. Invention also includes the finding of supporting materials for the topic. Arrangement is the process of organizing the materials in the speech to appropriately complete the speaking purpose. Style refers to selecting language suitable to the topic, occasion, and audience. Delivery is the canon describing how to present the speech. The final canon — memory — describes how to remember the speech. This canon is less important today than in ancient times when speakers had to prepare without benefit of pens, paper, or word processors.

This approach is systemic in the sense that a speech is an interrelationship of all the canons. If a speaker is competent in one canon, but not in others, the completed product will be unsatisfactory. A good speaker learns how to apply all the canons so the completed product is more than a "sum of the parts," but a "living" organism.

FIGURE 5.4 Rhetorical canons and mastery of the speech.

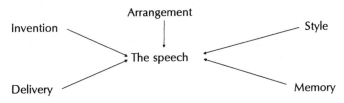

Teaching Individual Events from a Systems Perspective

The final subject this chapter discusses is the question of how we can apply the systems approach to teaching individual events. As noted earlier, this does not involve mastering formulas or learning only some aspects of speaking, but requires understanding all the systemic components of public speaking.

1. *Students must learn public speaking as a process.* A student needs to be involved in creating all parts of the speech. This may be done by viewing public speaking as a logical process that begins with considering the audience and occasion, then systematically creating the speech through the processes of invention, arrangement, style, and delivery.

2. *The role of the teacher is to guide the student through each step of the process.* The teacher should lay out the steps in the speaking process and help the students accomplish those steps. This includes several specific tasks. First, the teacher needs to instruct the students on process issues. The student needs to visualize speaking as a process rather than a product. Second, the teacher needs to supply the student with specific theories and models for each rhetorical canon. For instance, the teacher may keep a file of potential speech topics to help the student select a speech topic. Figure 5.5 lists specific suggestions for instruction in each of the canons.

The teacher can use any number of excellent public speaking textbooks for guiding speech preparation and practice. In this text, Chapter 8 discusses learning resources available to forensics teachers. The appendix at the end of this chapter gives an example of using the principles of invention in choosing oral interpretation selections for high school students.

Third, the teacher should emphasize practice. Because there is no single formula for learning public speaking, the single constant is the value of practice. Practice allows the student to experiment with new techniques and strategies. It is also an excellent opportunity for the teacher to provide constructive advice and criticism of the speaker and speech. The teacher can identify particular areas that the student can improve and provide suggestions for how the student can make these improvements. This will build the speaker's confidence so that she will be aware of what will be expected of her during the tournament.

Practice should emphasize more than simple repetition of speeches but should be constructive and systematic. The speaker should be instructed on areas needing improvement, and should receive reinforcement for successful behaviors. Improvement ought to be approached incrementally, where the speaker works on a single area of improvement before moving

FIGURE 5.5 Teaching suggestions for instruction using rhetorical canons.

CANON	SUGGESTION
Invention	Keep a file of potential topics. Keep a file with interpretation selections.
Arrangement	Create handouts with organizational patterns for speeches.
Style	Have sample speeches with different styles for study by students.
Delivery	Have students practice in front of a video camera to watch themselves speak. Have students critique each others' presentation.

on to another area. The teacher needs to create specific educational goals for each practice session. These would be similar to the lesson plans used in any regular classroom period.

Videotaping of speeches is a valuable practice tool. While students may initially be shy about watching themselves perform, this is a valuable way of instructing them on how to improve, for the student can see exactly the areas needing work.

SUMMARY

This chapter discusses teaching individual events. The first section analyzes the rationale for individual events in forensics education by suggesting a philosophy of individuals. The second section introduces the rules for commonly used individual events. The final section introduces a rhetorical perspective for teaching individual events emphasizing public speaking from a systems perspective using rhetorical canons of public speaking. (The next chapter provides a similar discussion for teaching and learning debate.) The appendix at the end of this chapter gives an example of using rhetorical principles and systems theory in helping high school students choose oral interpretation selections.

ACTIVITIES

1. Create a file of potential topics for various prepared speaking events. What are the characteristics of good topics? Would students be able to find sufficient information to develop a speech on the topic?

2. Write a five-minute speech for presentation to the class. The purpose can be either informative or persuasive. The speech should contain specific supporting material in the form of examples, quotations, or statistics. Discuss your speech with other class members and share ideas about the process of speech writing and the potential difficulties students encounter in writing speeches.

3. View a tape of a competitive public speech. What characteristics of the speech could be emphasized as good role models for other students? What parts of the speech seem to indicate use of the competitive speaking model? Does this detract from the overall success of the speech?

NOTES

1. David Mezzera and John Giertz, *Student Congress & Lincoln-Douglas Debate*, 2nd ed. (Lincolnwood: National Textbook, 1989). Gerald L. Ratliff, *Beginning Reader's Theatre: A Primer for Classroom Performance.* (Annandale: Speech Communication Assoc., 1981).

2. Sarah Trenholm, *Persuasion and Social Influence.* (Englewood Cliffs: Prentice Hall, 1969), Chapter 10.

3. Robert L. Scott and Bernard Brock. *Methods of Rhetorical Criticism: A Twentieth-Century Perspective.* (New York: Harper & Row, 1972). Sonja K. Foss, Rhetorical Criticism: Exploration and Practice. (Prospect Heights: Waveland, 1989). These are two of many useful books on the subject of rhetorical criticism. There is an excellent discussion of rhetorical criticism in a special edition of the *National Forensic Journal*, 3 (1985), Number 2.

4. Kristine M. Davis, "In Defense of the Value Oration." *The Forensic of Pi Kappa Delta*, 68 (1982): 602.

5. James A. Benson, "Extemporaneous Speaking: Organization Which Inheres." *Journal of the American Forensics Association, 14 (1978): 150–155.*

6. Albert A. Lord, *The Singer of Tales.* (New York: Atheneum, 1960).

7. Wallace A. Bacon, *The Art of Interpretation*, 2nd ed. (New York: Holt, Rinehart and Winston, 1972). Charlotte Lee, *Oral Interpretation*, 6th ed. (Boston: Houghton Mifflin, 1986).

8. Cf. Deborah Geisler, "Modern Interpretation Theory and Competitive Forensics: Understanding Hermeneutic Text." *National Forensic Journal*, 3 (1985): 71–79. Thomas G. Endres, "Maintaining Integrity in Forensics Interpretation: Arguments Against Original Literature." *National Forensic Journal*, 6 (1988): 89–102. Todd V. Lewis, "The Performance of Literature at Forensics Tournaments: A Case for the Use of Original Material;" Keith D. Green "Original Material in Forensics Oral Interpretation: A Violation of Integrity." *National Forensic Journal*, 6 (1988): 63–72.

9. George A. Kennedy, *Classical Rhetoric and Its Christian and Secular Tradition from Ancient to Modern Times.* (Chapel Hill: University of North Carolina Press, 1980).

APPENDIX TO CHAPTER 5

Finding Oral Interpretation Selections

The following brief article ("Finding Oral Interpretation Selections") was written by Virginia O'Keefe and published in the *Speech Communication Teacher*, Summer 1989, pp. 9–10.

Two questions keep recurring from speech coaches. Where does one find suitable material for oral interpretation, and once found, how should one prepare a program? The answers are not easy because both require time, effort, and individual considerations.

First, it is helpful if the material is not only of good quality, but relatively new. The language and subject should match the interpreter. A female can convey a female character's message more readily than a male. For instance, "Sixteen" by Maureen Daly, although dated in time, has a freshness of emotion with which teenage novice oral readers can identify. The student's familiarity with the situation immensely aids the reader's ability to relate it to an audience. Similar themes may be found by contemporary authors and can overcome a primary hurdle in interpretation: lack of background experience. Many of Ray Bradbury's stories of eerie science fiction are suitable for either sex. The major concerns are to find prose that contains action, dialogue, and some meaning that lingers in the judge's mind, even if a student is the first speaker in a round.

Stories usually are longer than the time limits allow. The National Forensic League has a 5 minute time limit for readings and the National Catholic Forensic League allows 10 minutes. Between these two extremes, various state and local tournaments and leagues set their own limitations. Usually, students can estimate they will read 150 words per minute. If the story is not too long, have your students read the whole text aloud at the appropriate speed while you time it. As you listen, note the parts that can be omitted without disrupting the meanings. Then estimate the number of words that must be eliminated and match that number with the portions that can be omitted.

95

Some slight tampering with the author's text, such as inserting an *and* or dropping *he said/she said/they said*, is permissible. Drastic alterations, which distort the text's meaning or emphasis, are unethical. For that reason, when students begin to cut their own texts, you should check the original manuscripts. Both the National Forensic League and the National Catholic Forensic League require contestants to have the original text and the complete source.

Poetry presents a different sort of challenge. Often, it is shorter than the time allowed. Therefore, a program of works by the same author, or on the same theme, may be arranged. An introduction and transitions generally should not exceed 30 seconds. For that reason, it is best to keep the poetry on a particular subject. Narrative, rather than descriptive poetry, is easier to interpret successfully. A listener hears the message only once, and without the luxury of rereading difficult passages, the effect can be lost. Poetry, as well as prose, should be selected for its narrative, dialogue, and emotional effect. Contemporary poetry is rich in imagery and impact and does not require a Barrymore expertise needed to deliver a Shakespearean sonnet, or Poe's "The Bells." Authors such as Sylvia Plath, Margaret Atwood, and James Dickey have an immediacy that students can grasp and perform well.

Finally, encourage your students to read, listen, and search for authors and works they enjoy. Once they have experienced the remarkable diversity of good competition, they will be motivated to discover their own favorites. That enthusiasm factor often is the unknown winning quality that we want to foster. Keep copies of everything your students perform and build a file. Next year's competition will be easier because of your team's effort this year.

6
Teaching Debate

This chapter is similar to the previous chapter in its coverage of individual events. It justifies debate as one of the traditional and most desirable educational learning tools. An educational philosophy of debate, again grounded in rhetorical principles, is introduced, the kinds of debate activities are outlined, and some specific teaching and learning techniques are offered.

Debate is the foundation of a free society. Since classical times, societies valuing democratic decision-making and free choice also have emphasized learning argumentation skills. It is more than coincidence that the nations with the longest uninterrupted tradition of democracy, the United States and Great Britain, have also nurtured the study and practice of academic debate. Other members of the British Commonwealth and, in recent years, Japan, have also encouraged students at schools and universities to participate in debate training.

The most systematic debate training for both high school and college students happens in the United States. Immigrants brought debate to the new world, and literary societies sustained it. Debate training flourished in schools and universities after its introduction into the formal educational curriculum around the beginning of the twentieth century. Competitive leagues were created and teachers were recruited to teach debate. Growing interest in teaching speech and debate led to creation of professional organizations, including what would become the Speech Communication Association, the largest professional organization of communication teachers. While not as popular as it once was, many high schools and colleges continue to support debate programs or teach debate classes.

This chapter discusses teaching and learning debate. As in Chapter 5, you will discover the educational philosophy of debate, the common kinds of debate activities, and the application of rhetorical principles to debate pedagogy.

THE PHILOSOPHY OF DEBATE

Debate flourishes when people care enough about their beliefs to risk them in confrontation but are not so intent on winning that they sacrifice their humanity or sense of fair play. Debate is more than a game. It is a system of structured learning that engages students to learn how to put aside their prejudices in favor of beliefs based on "good reasons." In creating a philosophical perspective of the debate activity we will consider the justification for learning debate, a philosophy of teaching debate, and the role of competition.

The Educational Values of Debate

Debate training predates the classical age of Athens. Earliest writing fragments date formal debate training at least to 476 B.C.[1] Debate training provided the impetus for the study of rhetoric, and scholars have considered debate useful as citizenship training since Aristotle's time. Debate was an integral part of classical rhetorical training in both Athens and Rome and later in England and the United States. The sheer longevity of debate training in education testifies to the belief that debate training is educationally valuable. It has been found that it provides people with four benefits: (1) Debate training teaches analysis and reasoning skills; (2) enhances research skills; (3) gives insight into public policy issues; and (4) provides the opportunity to improve oral communication abilities.

Debate teaches analysis and reasoning skills through teaching students how to create and refute arguments. Debate arguments range from very basic to highly complex and sophisticated. Even the most inexperienced debaters will make dozens of arguments in a debate, requiring students to exercise their analysis and research skills.

Debate also emphasizes good research skills and insight into public policy issues. Both high school and college debate programs use nationally selected resolutions. High school and college policy debate organizations use a single resolution for the entire year.[2] High school Lincoln-Douglas debate uses three topics, one for each quarter. These topics are generally the ones selected by the National Forensic League. The Cross-Examination Debate Association (CEDA) uses two topics, one for fall and the other for spring. Topic framers typically ground these resolutions in public policy concerns or, in Lincoln-Douglas debate, philosophical issues with implications for policy decisions.

Debate resolution authors attempt to create topics having two sides, with enough breadth for multiple interpretations of the topic. They do this to enhance research skills by requiring research of many case areas. This also leads to a better understanding of the topic itself.

Finally, debate also provides the opportunity to improve communication skills. Since students present debates orally to the judge or audience, they must master enough skill at speaking to transmit their arguments effectively.

While these benefits seem obvious when taken at face value, there is little consensus about their relative importance or how the debate activity ought to be structured to achieve them. Debate practice is split into three divergent schools of thought. Each of these perspectives emphasizes different philosophies and practices in debate. Each perspective is characterized by different "field variant characteristics."[3]

Critical-Thinking Perspective

The first perspective is that of *critical thinking*. This school of thought emphasizes the role of debate in building analysis and reasoning skills.[4] Debate skills are necessary ingredients to improving critical thinking abilities. Proponents of this view believe debate is a way of improving students' abilities at identifying and critiquing arguments.[5] Debate is, in this sense, a game that two people or teams play to develop and refute arguments.

The resolution, from this perspective, only creates the general topic area for the debate. The debaters are given very wide latitude in argument creation and the judge functions as a disinterested referee. The judge does not bring any preconceptions to the debate and decides the winner solely based on the arguments the debaters present. Delivery takes a decidedly secondary role, and arguments may be presented that have very little actual application to public policy concerns.

The field characteristics of debates using this perspective include fast delivery (sometimes called the "spread" strategy), heavy use of "global" arguments with limited application to the particular debate topic, and use of substantial amounts of debate evidence.

Public Speaking Perspective

The second perspective is that of *public speaking*. Rising primarily from dissatisfaction with perceived excesses of the critical-thinking perspective, this model views debate primarily as an opportunity to enhance communication skills through greater emphasis on delivery and less emphasis on evidence presentation and game playing.[6] This perspective evolved in the 1970s in both high school and college debate, and provided the impetus for creation of CEDA at the college level and reintroduction of Lincoln-Douglas as a national event at the high school level.

While new in the United States, this model is the predominant model in Great Britain and elsewhere. Under the title "Parliamentary Debate" or "Oxford Union Debate," British debaters have conducted public debates for centuries noted more for their audience-centered nature and less for their emphasis on analysis or evidence gathering.

The field characteristics of debates from this perspective include a significant audience orientation, including slower delivery, less emphasis on evidence presentation, and less use of issues in the debate.

Rhetorical Perspective

The third perspective is *rhetorical*. This model emphasizes a combination of both the critical-thinking and delivery-based models. This is the traditional perspective of most argumentation textbooks written since the 1950s.[7] The rhetorical perspective views debate as emphasizing equally the processes of analysis, research, and delivery. The purpose of the academic debate is to persuade the listener that one side did the better job of debating.

The field characteristics of debates using this perspective include being audience-centered, creating arguments using traditional argumentation elements, such as fallacies and tests of evidence, and striking a balance between evidence and delivery in the debate. Figure 6.1 diagrams the differences between these three perspectives.

Each of these perspectives has strengths and weaknesses. While any educator may prefer one over the other, we should emphasize the open nature of debate as a system. None of these perspectives dominates the debate landscape. Debaters will confront opponents and judges with differing views on the activity and must prepare for these diverse views. Failing to do so will lessen their chances for competitive and educational success.

FIGURE 6.1 Three perspectives about debate.

PERSPECTIVE	PURPOSE
Critical thinking	Making students better thinkers through increasing their creative abilities at creating and critiquing arguments.
Public speaking	Making students better public speakers through increasing their abilities to create appealing arguments in a competitive situation.
Rhetorical	Making students better communicators by learning both critical thinking and public speaking skills, but not emphasizing either exclusively.

This diversity of opinion about the nature and educational values of debate creates special challenges for debate teachers. Teachers must prepare students for debates where they have little advance knowledge about the philosophy of either their opponents or the judge. The teacher must create flexible arguers who are able to adapt well to uncertainty. This is the subject of the next section.

The Philosophy of Teaching Debate

Unlike teaching individual events, teaching debate requires background in and understanding of the debate process. It requires mastery of a new language, understanding of the structure of a debate, and insight into the situational elements of debates and debate tournaments. While this initially may seem daunting, observing and participating in debates quickly allows mastery of fundamentals and gradual understanding of more subtle nuances. There are several considerations that ought to guide the debate teacher.

1. *Students should create their own arguments and find their own evidence.*

Students should take primary responsibility for the invention process. This point was made in the previous chapter on individual events, but it strongly bears repeating here.

Debate can be viewed as a collaborative activity. Collaboration takes many forms. Debaters work with their debate partner to prepare arguments, and they may share their arguments or evidence with other team members. The debaters may use commercially produced evidence, collaborating with the producers of that evidence. The teacher also is a collaborator, critiquing the debaters and their preparation.

Collaboration is a useful benefit of debate and forensics training. There are few opportunities in life for people to work completely alone. Most work and social contexts require cooperative behaviors. Employers prize people who master cooperative skills in the job market and these people are likely to be more successful and happy.

Despite these benefits, there are several collaborative problems that we sometimes find in debates. The problem is not with collaborating itself, but how it is sometimes manifest in debates.

First, debaters sometimes rely on others to prepare their arguments or find their evidence. The final section of this chapter advocates that students share their evidence and ideas for arguments. Sometimes students take this to mean that it is acceptable for them to rely completely on the work of other students. If they are beginners they may feel inadequate as arguers or researchers. Of course, relying on other people does not help the student become a better arguer or researcher. Only working on those skills will improve them.

Second, debaters sometimes rely on commercially produced evidence or briefs instead of their own efforts. There are dozens of different debate handbooks sold commercially every year. These books contain evidence, articles analyzing the topic, and sometimes debate theory articles. Many high school policy debaters, in particular, rely heavily on handbooks to help them with their research and analysis.

There is justification for use of these sources. Debaters without access to good libraries may be disadvantaged in collecting evidence compared with debaters closer to college libraries or other good collections. Handbook evidence is usually collected by college debaters or high school or college teachers with extensive research experience. This sometimes means the evidence is much stronger than that collected by less experienced students. Finally, using handbooks is a way of being prepared for the kinds of arguments other competitors will make. The handbook may create a level playing field.

There also are disadvantages to handbooks. Relying exclusively on handbooks undermines learning the valuable research skills critical to the debate process. Handbooks also are expensive. Even if the school purchases them the cost still gives an advantage to the richer program, which may afford a greater number. Finally, handbooks are necessarily superficial. A handbook will not go into great depth on a particular topic. They sacrifice depth for breadth. The handbook producer cannot predict the directions a debate topic will take. They attempt to give the student some evidence on a wide range of topics.

Successful debate requires a much greater depth of understanding than handbooks can provide. They provide a useful service to beginning debaters by showing them what evidence is and how evidence may be used to create arguments. They help the more advanced debater find source citations for articles that may be helpful to them. But there is no justification for relying solely on the handbook as a substitute for library research. The increasing availability of computers and computerized distribution of information makes it likely that even the most geographically isolated debate program can find enough information to enjoy competitive success.

Third, teachers sometimes succumb to the temptation to intrude on the invention process by writing cases or researching arguments for students. The competitive pressure to be successful may explain such behavior. Students will sometimes create less sophisticated arguments than a teacher. Or they may pursue lines of argument that the teacher believes are undesirable. Drawing the line between collaboration and assuming primary responsibility for invention is one difficult problem facing forensics teachers.

It is both a competitive and an ethical problem. Condoning or encouraging students to rely on arguments created by others is no different than encouraging plagiarism or cheating.

2. *Students should strive for long-term instead of short-term benefits from debate.*

Any competitive context creates an incentive for sacrificing long-term understanding for immediate success. Debate is not different in this regard. Students tend to measure their success only in terms of the number of debates won, instead of the more intangible learning occurring.

Winning a debate and learning from participating in debate are not always synonymous. There are various shortcuts that increase the chances for immediate success that sacrifice long-term growth. Some visible shortcuts include rapid delivery, counter-intuitive arguments, and use of generic positions.

Incomprehensible delivery is the most consistent public criticism of the debate activity. Beginning in the 1960s delivery rates began a steep upward climb in both high school and college policy debate rounds. Normal conversational delivery is around 140 words per minute. One study of the final round of the National Debate Tournament calculated delivery speed to be nearly 300 words per minute.[8]

While most debates will not approach that extreme, rapid delivery remains a troubling characteristic of many debates and the subject of much concern.[9] There are several reasons for using this strategy.

First, debate has gradually become information-centered. We sometimes measure debate preparation in terms of quantity of evidence and arguments instead of their quality. This likely reflects an information oriented society where we are tempted to see information as power and over-rely on information in making decisions.[10]

A second reason for fast delivery is the belief that debate is critical-thinking and not rhetorically oriented. Believers of this view discount the importance of delivery, arguing that debate could nearly as easily be conducted through "written exchanges of briefs," and that oral delivery is merely a convenience.[11]

Finally, rapid delivery is also partially caused by the growing homogenization of debate judges. While rapid delivery became more fashionable, tournaments began to de-emphasize use of nontraditional judges in debate rounds. Tournament judging, with some exceptions, consists of people with debate training. Often these judges are recent competitors whose training in teaching and judging consists of nothing more than competitive experience. These judges, who learned rapid delivery and the concomitant ability to understand such a technique, expect debaters to conform to the expectation of speaking quickly.

This is one of the most troubling and paradoxical systemic characteristics of contemporary debate. It is paradoxical in the sense that on the one hand we encourage debaters to adapt to their audience and on the other hand give them a very narrow range of audiences they need to consider.

Criticism of rapid delivery focuses on the inapplicability of the skill in other arguing contexts. Anecdotal evidence suggests debaters have to "unlearn" rapid delivery skills when speaking elsewhere. Critics also suggest that such delivery skills are inhumane to listeners.[12] Unfortunately, no empirical study documents the seemingly inescapable relation of declining participation in debate and increasing delivery rates in recent years.

A second problem is reliance on counter-intuitive, arguments in debate. A *counter-intuitive argument* is one that goes against common sense or the general state of knowledge. Fear of teaching counter-intuitiveness is one of the oldest criticisms of educational debate. Political leaders and scholars in the early twentieth century all feared teaching students to argue against their principles by debating both sides of the resolution. While that particular controversy died out long ago, it has been replaced by the same conflict in another form. This current dispute focuses on the practice of using arguments with questionable causal links but extremely significant impact. For example:

> Advertising portrays harmful images of non-Western people. North Korean leaders watch American television advertisements and conclude that American society is prejudiced against them. This causes them to escalate tensions in Korea and will ultimately lead to nuclear conflict.

This argument is, at best, questionably causal. Unfortunately, there is a trend in debate toward debating the impact instead of the causality of these arguments. This creates contexts where judges decide debate winners by comparing the number of "dead bodies" stacked up in the round.

Defenders sometimes justify these practices by considering debate as a laboratory for experimenting with arguments even if those arguments seem initially far-fetched, while disregarding the superficiality of a debate. The time limits of any debate prevents deep and complex arguing on even the most obvious arguments suggested by the resolution. Counter-intuitive arguments, requiring many causal links to establish them, are even less likely to be adequately developed in the debate.

A third problem is the increasing reliance on generic, theory-based arguments in debates. Many debates revolve around theory arguments instead of the substantive issues concerned uniquely with the resolution.

Using this approach, the debater writes briefs on a theoretical position and applies that position to whatever affirmative case confronts her. The short-term utility of this approach comes from narrowing the range of potential arguments the debater needs to prepare for.

Current examples of generic arguments include issues such as: topicality, intrinsicality, hasty generalizations, one-line definitions of terms, counter-warrants, and language-based feminism positions. The exact nature of these arguments constantly evolves and depends in part on the exact wording of the debate resolution.

The main criticism of the strategy of using generic arguments in debate is its role in divorcing debate from analysis of the substantive issues suggested by the debate resolution. Instead of focusing the debate on the usual stock issues, the debate revolves around these artificial and highly theoretical arguments that depend heavily on academic debate theory. Many of these arguments lack more general applicability to other arguing contexts.

In summary, rapid delivery, counter-intuitive, and theory-based arguments are common situational elements of many debates. These strategies emphasize winning the debate as an end and do not prepare the debater for other arguing contexts.

3. *Students should participate in multiple events.*

Participating in debate alone is probably insufficient to teach students all the skills they need to maximize their experience in forensics. No form of debate, including high school Lincoln-Douglas, will teach speech delivery skills sufficiently to prepare students for the speaking contexts they will encounter. Debate training introduces skills that must be refined and developed through internalization. Students internalize skills through applying them broadly.

Students best internalize debate skills through applying them outside the debate round. Combining an active competitive program with audience debating, individual events, and public speaking encourages students to look at forensics more holistically, or as citizenship training instead of a game to be mastered.

To summarize this section, the philosophy of teaching debate is guided by three needs: (1) The teacher must allow the students to be the primary inventor of their arguments. (2) The teacher must teach in ways that encourage students to achieve long-term benefits instead of simply short-term success. (3) The teacher also must view competitive debate as just one part of the larger educational experience. Students need to prepare in other events to derive the full benefits of forensics training.

The Role of Competition in Debate

One of this text's common themes is the complex and sometimes inconsistent relation between competition and education. The inherent difficulty of learning successful debate illustrates this problem. It is not difficult to learn debate fundamentals. Brief study is all that is necessary to master speaker order and basic arguing techniques. It is difficult, however, to become a consistently successful winner in competitive debate.

Success in competitive debate requires mastering many situational variables, such as creating briefs, understanding debate theory, arguing against unexpected cases, and analyzing judges. Furthermore, experience is virtually the only way to learn about these situational constraints. The teacher can discuss theoretical issues but cannot anticipate how arguing in a particular debate will affect those issues.

The major value of debate competition is its role in motivating students to broaden their arguing, analysis, and research skills. Healthy competition is fun and the particular motivational structure of debate tournaments often reinforces the enjoyable aspects of competition. Dividing students into ability groups, power-matching to ensure that debaters are not consistently overmatched, and giving awards for success all help motivate students to try to improve their skills and reach their potential as arguers.

There also is, however, a downside to competition. As observed earlier, competitive pressure may cause students to focus on short-term instead of long-term goals. They may see winning the debate as the end and not the means to learn new and valuable skills.

Students doubtlessly ought to focus on long-term rather than short-term goals. Unfortunately, they probably will not readily understand that goal. The teacher must constantly monitor progress toward long-term goals and discourage practices designed solely for short-term benefit.

This section examines the justification for debate training. It outlines the common reasons for learning debate, an educational philosophy of teaching debate, and a brief orientation to the role of competition in debate training. The next section outlines the common kinds of debate activity.

THE TYPES OF DEBATE ACTIVITIES

Compared with individual events, debate activities are considerably more limited in number. We compensate for limited event numbers through greater variety in how debate events are performed. High schools and colleges, for example, use the same kinds of debate rules but often debate very differently, as do different sections of the United States. In other words, the situational elements of debate provide the variety lacking from just considering the structural elements.[13] This contrasts with the previous discussion of individual events, where the structural differences in individual events are probably more significant than the situational elements.

There are four major debate types: team policy, team value, Lincoln-Douglas, and parliamentary style. As you will see shortly, their differences lie more in situational rather than structural differences.

Team Policy Debate

Team policy debate is the oldest form of academic debate. The major defining feature of team policy debate is use of a policy resolution ("Resolved: That the United States should adopt a comprehensive system of medical care for all U. S. citizens"). Policy debaters typically present a plan and focus the debate over issues relating to policy concerns.

Team Value Debate

This contrasts with team policy debate. This form of debate uses a value-oriented resolution ("Resolved: That guaranteeing medical care to all U. S. citizens would benefit this nation"). Value debaters typically discuss criteria for accepting a value claim and compare that value to competing values.

Lincoln-Douglas Debate

Lincoln-Douglas debate dates from World War II, but gained popularity in the 1970s with its adoption as an official event by the National Forensic League.[14] Named after the famous encounters between Abraham Lincoln and Stephen Douglas, advocates envisioned Lincoln-Douglas debate as an alternative to the perceived excesses of team policy debate.

The high school Lincoln-Douglas format uses value-oriented resolutions that change several times during the debate season. Debaters are encouraged to use less evidence and be more communicative in their style, as well as use different strategies and arguments than found in team policy debate.

Parliamentary Debate

Parliamentary debate is the fourth major type of competitive debate. This form of debate, closely modeled after Oxford Union Debate practiced in

British colleges, is less structured than the other commonly used forms. This form of debate may use either policy or value resolutions and allows for greater audience involvement and less emphasis on use of evidence and complex argument. Because parliamentary debate is not widely used in the United States, we will not consider this form of debate in the rest of this chapter. There are tournaments, however, that use a parliamentary form and it could become more popular.

The Elements of Debate

Debate combines both structural and situational elements. Figure 6.2 lists some important structural characteristics of debates.

These are the only structural constraints commonly present in debate. This makes debate, at one level, almost elegantly simple in structure. Presumably, it is simple enough for a beginner to learn quickly and participate in successfully. This structural simplicity probably attracted teachers toward debate in the first place.

Over the years debate moved away from simple structure toward greater complexity through adoption of more complex situational constraints. Situational debate elements are those parts of debate connected with the actual debate context, as opposed to the formal rules that characterize the structural debate elements. Figure 6.3 lists some current situational elements of debate.

Each of these situational elements will be different in each level of debate (high school or college), type of debate (policy, value, or Lincoln-Douglas), and individual debate tournament and round.

Decision-rules refer to the standards for evaluating issues in a debate. Decision-rules are usually debatable issues and are often connected with either theoretical or substantive issues. The original form of decision-rules were "stock issues."[15] Greek rhetoricians identified some issues that, by their inherent nature, would be considered by an audience in deciding the outcome of any dispute.

FIGURE 6.2 Structural characteristics of debate.

1. Time limits and specific debate format. All academic debate formats specify speaking time-limits and the order of the speeches.
2. Use of a specified debate resolution. The resolution specifies the issues and subjects participants will debate, so that they know what to prepare.
3. Use of a judge who gives a decision about which side or speaker won the debate. The judge listens to the debate and provides comments both about the style and substance of the debaters.

FIGURE 6.3 Situational elements of debate.

1. Decision rules for determining decisions. Different formats emphasize different issues important for determining which side wins a debate.
2. Judging paradigms. There are various judging models or paradigms available to help the debate judge in evaluating debates.
3. Jargon and context-bound language. Both the nature of debate and subject matter influence language choices that differentiate debates from other arguing contexts.
4. Debate conventions. Debate conventions include informal rules and norms commonly used in debates.

Stock issues became the basis of legal decision-making, particularly as a part of English Common Law. These legal stock issues probably were borrowed in early debate textbooks for use in academic debate. Early textbooks suggest the stock issues for policy debate include "significance," "inherency," and "workability." Another system suggested "ill," "blame," "cure," and "cost."

Gradually, other decision-rules emerged. When the comparative advantage case format became popular during the 1960s, workability expanded to include "disadvantages versus advantages." Topicality also became recognized as a stock issue. Some critics observe that the stock issue of inherency has lost favor as counter-intuitive arguments became more popular. These arguments stressed the issue of significance and de-emphasized the possibilities that existing mechanisms may obviate the problem.

The growing popularity of value debate also affected use of decision-rules. There is no consensually shared system of stock issues for value debate. Stock issues in policy debate were originally grounded in legal stock issues. No corresponding system seemed to fit value debate, particularly in its early use. This contributed to a sense of theoretical fuzziness about judging value debates. Scholars have recently introduced different decision-making systems without creating, thus far, agreement about which system is most useful.[16]

Another recent addition to debate theory is interest in judging paradigms. Judging paradigms refer to the model the judge uses to evaluate the debate round. Paradigms such as the "policy maker," "hypothesis tester," "agenda-setter," or "critic of argument" emerged to give judges some choices about how they view debates.

Before the 1960s, most judges looked at debates in the same way. They considered themselves debate skills evaluators or possibly used the stock issues as their guides. These models strongly emphasized delivery skills and analysis. Widespread acceptance of these models meant that debates were usually similar to each other. The 1960s introduced new models, such as the policy-making and hypothesis-testing models that opened debates to a much wider range of acceptable models. This trend has continued to the present. There are many paradigms (as discussed in Chapter 7), and no one model dominates judging. This makes judge adaptation a very crucial situational demand on debaters.

A third situational element is increasing use of specialized language in debate. Jargon is not, of course, unique to debate. Every discipline has its own language system. A person comparing the language in professional journals in communication, for example, would see considerable differences in just the last 30 years. Specialized language often allows for greater precision in describing phenomena. Sometimes, unfortunately, it merely confuses understanding.

Which effect results from an increased reliance on specialized language in debate is, in itself, a debatable proposition. Despite its desirability, jargon is inevitably a part of debate. This means that a student wishing to be successful must master the specialized language of debate in addition to understanding the often specialized language of the debate subject area.

A taxonomy of debate jargon would be long and probably soon dated. It would include many of the terms discussed in this chapter that presume familiarity with argumentation concepts. Some of these terms include: *topicality, intrinsicness, turn-arounds, case-flips, permutations*, and *d-rules,* just a few of the many linguistic terms debaters need to master.

The final situational element is the importance of debate conventions; or customs. Every communication context includes considerable demand for conventional behavior. Scholars group explanations of behavioral conventions in communication under the title "rules theory."[17] Rules theory suggests that people structure their world in part by communicating according to certain prescriptions about what is "preferable or necessary." This perspective is obvious. We teach children communication conventions, such as turn-taking and language rules, at a very early age. As we grow older, we learn rules about communicating with teachers, members of the opposite sex, and employers. Like other contexts, debate has its own conventions.

These conventions are fluid. Some are common sense. Common sense conventions include politeness and respect for opponents and judges. Other conventions, including dress and delivery speed, are not as universally accepted. A norm in one place may be unacceptable in another. We face this challenge in every communicative situation.

A final comment about conventions is in order. This discussion should not be interpreted to mean that debate ought to be approached strictly from a situational perspective. The role of the teacher is to articulate some particular educational standards that should be absolute. A teacher who strongly dislikes fast delivery, for example, should not be required to compromise that view in order to accept a competing viewpoint. The teacher must determine what conventions he chooses to help his students conform to, and which he rejects. Doing so obviously is risky, since students may lose an occasional debate, but is highly important for the teacher to maintain a sense of perspective between achieving short-term and long-term goals.

In summary, this section describes debate activities. There are four primary debate types: team policy, team value, Lincoln-Douglas, and parliamentary debate. In distinguishing debate types we examine both structural and situational variables. The situational variables are the most important in understanding debate practice. The situational variables include use of decision-rules, judging paradigms, specialized language, and communication conventions. The final section of this chapter looks at some teaching strategies for debate.

TEACHING AND LEARNING STRATEGIES FOR DEBATE

Our perspective on teaching and learning strategies will be very similar to our discussion in Chapter 5. There is no single way to teach or learn debate. As a highly intellectual activity, it cannot be reduced to a series of formulas or "plays." Every debate will be a unique experience with arguments and strategies different from other debates.

The rhetorical approach we discussed in Chapter 5 is an appropriate model for teaching debate. Teachers of rhetoric first used debate to teach rhetorical principles. Early teachers used techniques called "suasoria" and "controversia" to help students create appropriate arguments for different contexts and to practice arguing those positions orally.[18]

A rhetorically grounded approach must, of course, adapt to the unique situational elements of contemporary debate. Debaters in classical Athens or Rome faced homogeneous audiences, narrow resolutions, and far less information than a high school or college debate student of today. Simply telling a student "go to the library and research the topic, and then write your case . . . ," although spiritually consistent with classical training, would cause the student considerable frustration and failure. Instead, while emphasizing simplicity and the need for the student to take responsibility for the arguing process, the teacher must use strategies and theories that will create greater likelihood for student success.

The rest of this section suggests five theoretical perspectives that the teacher needs to consider in helping students to achieve competitive success in debate. Not all have obvious antecedents to classical theories. They do sketch a starting place for the teacher to develop a teaching philosophy adapted to her particular program and teaching beliefs.

Uncertainty Reduction

Uncertainty reduction is a useful approach to understanding human communicative behavior. The premise is that people are motivated to increase the predictability of communicative situations and avoid or adapt uncertain situations to be consistent with their beliefs. Uncertainty leads to being uncomfortable about communicating. We are shy, for example, about talking to a new acquaintance that we do not know very much about.

Uncertainty pervades the debate context. The debater must research and prepare arguments on an unfamiliar subject. They must work with a partner or another squad member whose skills and motives may be unknown. They will debate another team or person without knowing what precise arguments or strategies their opponent will introduce in front of a judge who could be a stranger.

The teacher's most important job is addressing uncertainty and helping the student to understand and adapt to various uncertain situations. The teacher may do this in several ways.

First, the teacher should instruct the debaters on the format of debates and the various situational elements they will encounter. Observing debates before participating in them would be one way of accomplishing this end. This is contrary to the notion of letting a student "sink or swim" by thrusting him unprepared into a debate. This is likely to be unsuccessful because the student will be caught up in the uncertainty of the situation. The teacher also should carefully read ballots and debrief students after the tournament about their experiences.

Second, the teacher should strongly encourage research and not rely on handbooks or pre-prepared evidence. Research is valuable because students learn the underlying premises of the arguments they make. They understand the issues in greater depth, which helps them understand and respond to opposing arguments. Similarly, the student should not present briefs, cases, or arguments developed by other students or teachers. While giving beginning students cases and briefs to read seems appealing, it may actually cause greater uncertainty-induced anxiety.

Third, the teacher should emphasize collaborative learning techniques. Debate is an excellent context for teaching collaboration. Working with other debaters on research, case writing, or practice debating emphasizes that debate need not be a lonely pursuit. A persistent myth of debate is the picture of the solitary debater working alone in the library for long hours and then triumphing solely through the power of her superior arguments. While there surely are debaters successful this way, they are the exception. Debate success more likely will come from collaboration. Debate collaboration takes many forms. For example, debaters can use central evidence files to share their team's research burden. Having other students double-check the accuracy of source citations and evidence context also will teach good research skills. Debaters also can work together to devise arguments or responses to arguments they expect may occur.

Fourth, and finally, the teacher should teach students about the nature of uncertainty and its effects on behavior. Teaching students to expect uncertainty and how it can influence their debate success may in itself inoculate the students and prepare them for other unanticipated situations.

Source Credibility and Audience Adaptation

Aristotelian theory strongly emphasizes *ethos* and audience adaptation as crucial persuasive elements. Ethos is only one of three forms of proof in Aristotle's system, but it is the form that seems to receive less attention from students. This is due to a perspective of debate that places the audience in a subordinate position to the debaters. We discussed this perspective (critical-thinking model) earlier in the chapter. This theory emphasizes the judge as a referee and not as a participant.

The fundamental weakness of this perspective is, of course, its estrangement from the real-world contexts of argument. The truth that Aristotle recognized two thousand years ago is still most applicable. In contexts outside academic debate rounds, arguers must consider themselves as a form of proof and must consider the judge or listener as an active participant in the process.

There are a myriad of communication studies on source credibility. Persuasion textbooks discuss them in greater detail.[19] While these studies identify many source credibility variables, they identify factors that debaters can consider. Discussion of credibility elements is itself a valuable educational tool. It ought to help the student understand how audiences behave and respond to messages.

Emphasizing audience adaptation is a skill that even an inexperienced debate teacher can teach successfully. Students can learn the various debate judging paradigms and apply those paradigms to judges they see in tournaments. They can compare the strategies and styles necessary to persuade inexperienced audiences with those necessary to succeed with highly trained listeners. This learning should encourage debaters to become flexible and provisional arguers, thus becoming more "rhetorically sensitive."[20]

Games Theory

Debate is an example of using game playing to teach skills. This is common educational practice. Chess, for instance, developed as a way of teaching war strategy. Games teach children turn-taking, problem-solving, and even counting skills. Computer games help students learn math, spelling, and even world geography. We use them because they work.

While some game elements of debate are undesirable, others help students learn skills and accomplish objectives the students may otherwise not achieve. In its most general sense, the game of debate encourages students to research and argue in systematic ways they would otherwise not choose to do.

The teacher's role in this regard is two-fold. First, the teacher must help the student understand and apply game elements in debate. It was described in the prior section as the situational elements of debate. Students must understand debate language, debate theories, and debate customs. This emphasizes both the teacher and student as observers. Like the anthropologist studying a previously unknown civilization, the teacher and debater must observe and decide why some debaters are successful and others are not. This judgment should not be solely based on finding students who win but rather students who win while using educationally appropriate strategies and styles.

Observation is an important way of building game-related skills. Chess players replay famous games to understand strategies of master players. They learn that master chess players think several moves ahead and have a game plan for every match. A debater can observe other debaters to gain insight into the reasons for their success. For example, students eliminated from a tournament ought to watch other elimination rounds to compare strategies. Inexperienced debaters ought to find role models of successful debaters they can emulate. They should not become clones of others, but should integrate certain behaviors into their own debate style.

The second role of the teacher is to emphasize context in game-related activity. The teacher needs to help the student develop perspective. The teacher must not let the student get carried away by the game to the detriment of the larger vision of debate. As discussed, this is very easy for students to do and much harder for teachers to remedy.

Motivation

Debate demands substantial ego involvement. As in sports or other competitive forms, risking one's self-image through forensics competition can be difficult. There is a natural tendency to take defeat personally and over-emphasize the significance of defeat. The structure of competitive debate ensures that everyone will lose debate rounds occasionally and that every student probably will receive critical feedback from judges. The reverse, of course, is also true—students will win debates and receive positive feedback. Another function of teaching debate is involvement in student motivation.

There is a degree of "self-selection bias" regarding students choosing to participate in debate. Debate likely attracts students who have strong egos and high levels of self-motivation.[21] Even so, motivation is still an important part of competitive debate. The teacher has several functions in student motivation.

First, the teacher suggests goals and expectations for competitors. The teacher needs to define success operationally for students. He needs to balance the skills of the student with achievable goals. Telling a novice student "your goal is winning the state tournament" could likely be unrealistic, particularly if the program does not have the necessary resources to pursue that goal. But the teacher also needs to set goals that are beyond the easy reach of the student, to motivate them to improve.

Second, the teacher must instill personal goals and competitive goals. The teacher needs to identify ways each student can improve personally and competitively. The function of the program is not just to win awards but to educate citizens. Students should have goals that relate to their personal improvement (for example, becoming a better listener) and their competitive improvement. Periodically reviewing these goals can help the student and teacher keep competition in perspective.

Third, the teacher must be a good motivational role model. Teaching debate also involves a teacher's ego. A teacher can take winning and losing debates just as personally as students. We often see sports coaches succumb to this problem. You may remember the legendary college basketball coach Bobby Knight throwing a chair across the court a few years ago. A debate teacher is just as likely as a basketball coach to do this.

Your educational training probably has stressed the need to balance positive and negative reinforcement of students. This may contrast with your experiences in sports or other competitive contexts. There are all too many "Little League Parents," for example, who teach through intimidation and negative reinforcement. On the other hand, failing to help students understand what aspects of their debating needs improvement also would be undesirable. It could cause them to lose interest, believing they were just not very good at debate.

Internalization of Learning Outcomes

Debate's ultimate value is preparing students for wider argumentation contexts. This requires the student to internalize her knowledge and skills so she can apply that knowledge in future situations.

Some internalization happens inevitably, regardless of encouragement. The teacher can, however, stimulate internalization in several ways.

Students should learn debate skills incrementally. The magnitude of skills necessary for competitive success can appear threatening. The beginning student should work on improving one or two skills at a time. Repetition will improve the overall skill level and identifying one or two areas to improve helps the student focus on the value of those skills and how they can be learned.

Teachers should find opportunities for debate beyond the competitive domain. The time that the student learns particular skills is the ideal time to encourage his internalization through application in other areas. An active campus, school audience debate program, or even simply encouraging participation in campus or school political organizations can help lead to internalization.

Lastly, *programs should verbalize the importance of internalization.* Teachers can discuss the applicability of skills in other contexts and remind students of the need to apply their new skills in new areas. This is consistent with a program philosophy emphasizing debate and speech as a means rather than just competitive ends.

SUMMARY

This chapter discusses teaching debate. The first section explores the educational values of debate—why students learn it and what an appropriate educational philosophy of debate teaching may involve. The second section examines the structure of debate, including the commonly used events and the importance of situational constraints on understanding debate. The third section introduces some debate teaching techniques.

This is the second of three chapters in the text devoted to systems of forensics pedagogy, covering individual events and debate as teaching forms. These pedagogical chapters conclude with Chapter 7 by looking at the third teaching venue, tournament judging.

ACTIVITIES

1. Watch an academic debate, either live or on tape. Analyze the skills needed for success. Keep a list of comments you would make to the speakers about improving their skills. Keep another list of all the conventions you observe the students following.
2. Interview some debaters about things they like or dislike about debate. Ask them about the good and bad points about practices and actual tournament rounds. How would they change debates or tournaments to be more fun and educational?
3. Keep a list of debate jargon terms you encounter. Compare your list with others in class. Find definitions for those terms and share your definitions with ones generated by other students. Keep the best definitions for your file.

NOTES

1. James J. Murphy, *A Synoptic History of Classical Rhetoric*. (New York: Random House, 1972).
2. In high school debate, the national policy topic is chosen by the National Federation of State High School Activity Associations topic committee. In college, a topic selection committee consisting of members of several organizations writes a topic used by schools participating in NDT debate. (See Chapter 2 for further information on the structure of high school and college debate.)
3. One useful perspective of argumentation is to consider arguments as they occur in argument "fields." Examples of argument fields are legal argument, or competitive forensics. In applying a field perspective we examine "field variant" and "field invariant" characteristics. Field variant characteristics are ones that are unique to the particular argument field.
4. See previously cited article by A. C. Snyder. Edward Panetta, "A Rationale for Developing a Nationally Competitive National Debate Tournament Oriented Program." *Argumentation and Advocacy*, 27 (1990): 68–77.
5. Kent R. Colbert, "The Effects of CEDA and NDT Debate Training on Critical Thinking Ability." *Journal of the American Forensic Association*, 23 (1987): 194–201.
6. See previously cited articles by Jack Howe and Richard Hunsaker.
7. Douglas Ehninger and Wayne Brockriede, *Decision by Debate*. (New York: Dodd, Mead, 1963). Glen Mills, *Reason in Controversy*. (Boston: Allyn and Bacon, 1963). Austin J. Freeley, *Argumentation and Debate*, 6th ed. (Belmont: Wadsworth, 1986).
8. Kent R. Colbert, "Speaking Rates of N.D.T. Finalists from 1968–1980." *Journal of the American Forensic Association*, 18 (1981): 73–76.
9. See discussion in Donn Parson, ed., *American Forensics in Perspective*. (Annandale: Speech Communication Assoc., 1984), Chapter 5.

10. Alvin Toffler, *Future Shock*. (New York: Bantam Books, 1971).

11. Beverly Kelly, "An Alternative to NDT Debate." *CEDA Yearbook 1981: The Philosophy and Practice of CEDA*, pp. 8–14.

12. David A. Frank, "Delivery and Debate." Presented to CEDA Assessment Conference, St. Paul, MN, 1991.

13. Bartanen and Frank, *Debating Values*, Chapter 2.

14. Hunsaker, *Lincoln-Doublas Debate: Defining and Judging Value Debate*.

15. Stock issues are points of dispute that must be resolved before accepting a policy, fact, or value. Argumentation and debate theorists adopted the concept of stock issues for use in debate.

16. There are a number of models that have been introduced. Walter Ulrich, "Philosophical Systems as Paradigms for Value Debate." *CEDA Yearbook* (1983), pp. 22–28. Michael Bartanen and David Frank, "The Issue-Agenda Model." *The Forensic*, 69 (1983): 1–9. Jeffrey Bile, "When the Whole Is Greater than the Sum of the Parts: The Implications of Holistic Resolutional Focus," *CEDA Yearbook* (1987), pp. 8–15.

17. Susan Shimanoff, *Communication Rules: Theory and Research*. (Beverly Hills: Sage, 1980)

18. Kennedy, *Classical Rhetoric and Its Christian and Secular Tradition from Ancient to Modern Times*. M. L. Clarke, *Higher Education in the Ancient World*. (London: Routledge and Kegan Paul, 1971).

19. Charles U. Larson, *Persuasion: Reception and Responsibility*, 6th ed. (Belmont: Wadsworth, 1992).

20. Roderick Hart and Don Burks, "Rhetorical Sensitivity and Social Interaction." *Communication Monographs*, 39 (1972): 75–91.

21. Evidence for this claim is anecdotal. There are few studies analyzing the motivational characteristics of debate students.

7
Judging Forensics Contests

The final element of the educational domain is the teaching and learning done in connection with contest judging. In some ways, this is one of the most important teaching concepts to master. The judge is the teacher who has the ability to give immediate feedback to students to improve their competitive and educational performance. This chapter discusses the three roles the judge performs—educator, facilitator, and trustee. Specific technical aspects of judging are also outlined. The chapter concludes by discussing methods that teachers and competitors can use to study ballots after the tournament.

One anomaly of forensics is that very frequently teachers have more contact with students from other schools than they do with their own. The competing demands of teaching and administering a program prevent teachers from spending as much time coaching their own students as they might like. At the tournament, they will judge many rounds while their students are competing. They will have very few opportunities to talk with their students between rounds. Instead, they will spend much energy judging other students and giving those students constructive criticism of their performance. It is this educational function that is the subject of this chapter.

Judging is the last of the subsystems of the educational domain to be examined. Judging is both the easiest and most difficult teaching activity. It is easy in the sense that basic judging techniques are simply mastered. Knowing the skills, however, does not ensure judging competency. A competent judge listens carefully, is impartial, and is educationally minded. The judge must develop these skills just like any other teaching skill. This chapter covers two subjects—the educational philosophy of forensics judging and the practical considerations of judging competitive debate and public speaking rounds.

THE EDUCATIONAL PHILOSOPHY OF JUDGING

The educational rationale for judging forensics events may not be as self-evident as for the other subsystems of teaching forensics. There are many college and high school teachers who do not judge at tournaments. This might be a growing trend. They prefer to coach their own students or to help run the tournament. Other teachers feel they are not competent judges or may dislike the characteristics of competitive rounds or events. While these concerns are valid they should not take precedence over judging as a crucial educational activity.

Why is judging so important? Judging is the crucial educational medium of the forensics contest as an educational form. The judge observes the students in action as competitors and learners. They set the educational standards the students try to meet. They give the most immediate feedback about performance that may profoundly affect the student's future behaviors. The judge performs three essential roles in meeting these responsibilities: educator, facilitator, and trustee of the activity. Figure 7.1 lists the skills and activities connected to each of these roles.

The Judge as Educator

The basic function of the judge is critiquing the speakers' performances in the contest events. This is the same role the teacher plays in the classroom. The competitive individual events or debate round is, in this sense, a classroom where we expect the teacher to set educational goals and standards and give feedback to students about their performance.

We expect the forensics judge to meet the same standards as the classroom teacher or professor. They are expected to have a clearly articulated

FIGURE 7.1 Activities connected to roles performed by the forensics contest judge.

1. Judge as educator
   - Develops a philosophy or paradigm for judging.
   - Applies that philosophy consistently and makes sure students know the philosophy and how it is applied.

2. Judge as facilitator
   - Must understand and apply contest rules.
   - Must write constructive comments.
   - Must help tournament run smoothly.

3. Judge as trustee
   - Monitors and enforces ethical standards.

activist educational philosophy, to have a constructive perspective about criticism, and to have a genuine interest in the growth and well being of students.

The judge should have a clearly articulated activist educational philosophy. Like the teacher, he should understand what they are trying to accomplish while judging. The judge needs to articulate his perspective about what a good speech or debate entails and what behaviors are appropriate for the contest round. A successful teacher is not a passive reactant to students but an active agent in helping students learn.

The judge's educational philosophy takes the form of a "judging paradigm." The paradigm is the model the judge uses to evaluate both the content and process of debating and speaking. There are many paradigms judges can choose from. (Several of these paradigms are examined later in this chapter.)

Similarly, the judge is not a passive observer but an agent of change in the competitive round. There is considerable controversy regarding the appropriateness of judges as active agents in the conduct of the competitive round. One point of view, discussed in Chapter 6 as the critical-thinking perspective of debate, identifies the judge as a passive agent, reacting to the presentation of the students. This view believes that the judge should not impose standards of presentation or argument on students but allow the students maximum freedom of choice.

This view is difficult to reconcile with the role of a judge as an educator. A successful classroom instructor is not a passive reactant but an active agent in creating learning. The teacher should not impose her views on students, but neither should she merely react. The best outcomes occur when both teachers and students work together to establish a learning environment. This is also true in the forensics contest round. The best learning environment occurs when both teachers and students take responsibility for the learning process.

One change in judging in recent years is increasing acceptance of judges presenting oral judging philosophies and discussing the round with students after its completion. An oral judging philosophy, especially for debate rounds, is a useful educational tool. It helps students understand and prepare to adapt to those expectations. The judge must, however, be sensitive in presenting an oral judging philosophy to recognize the difficulties she might cause the debaters or speakers. The philosophy should be provisional, not precluding students from making arguments or speaking in ways that are inconsistent with the philosophy. The judging philosophy ought to be a guide, not an inflexible guarantee of how the judge will view the contest round.

Many judges also discuss the round with the competitors after its completion. This too can be useful, if handled correctly. The judge should not discuss the decision of who won with the students, for two reasons: (1) This discussion could cause a confrontation between the speakers and the judge. An inexperienced judge may feel intimidated. (2) It may not be in a competitor's best interest to know exactly how well he is doing. Students respond to that knowledge in different ways. Knowing they are doing poorly, for example, could discourage some students and motivate others to improve. Some teachers, as part of their program philosophy, may prefer that their students not know the information.

The major value of post-round discussion is the chance to provide immediate feedback about performance. Interpersonal communication is superior to written communication in this regard. The judge may not feel free to write all the comments he wishes to make or may forget to write them in the rush to get to his next round. Discussing the judge's perceptions also gives the student the opportunity to take those into account during the tournament instead of having to wait until the tournament is over.

In summary, as an educator, the judge must develop a clear learning philosophy to apply in judging. This philosophy should allow the judge to actively participate in the contest learning environment. The judge can use techniques such as presenting an oral judging philosophy before the round or discussing the round with the student to improve the feedback process.

The Judge as Facilitator

The second role of the judge is to facilitate the forensics contest by ranking and rating speakers and rendering decisions in the debate round. This is the most visible function of the judge and the function requiring training. Judges untrained in appropriate judging practices disrupt the smooth functioning of the tournament and are unlikely to give helpful feedback to competitors.

The facilitation function has three elements. The judge must (1) understand and follow the contest rules, (2) write constructive comments, and (3) help the tournament run smoothly.

The first aspect of facilitation is understanding and following the contest rules. Forensic contests involve two dimensions, substantive elements and contest elements. Figure 7.2 describes the differences between substantive and contest elements.

Substantive elements refer to the content dimensions of the speech or debate. The substantive elements include the "artistic proofs" of the speaking act. The *contest dimensions* are the "inartistic" proofs, and those unique

FIGURE 7.2 Substantive and contest elements of forensics contests.

SUBSTANTIVE ELEMENTS
The "content" of the speech or debate.
Includes the use of evidence, types of claims, organizational
and presentational elements of individual speeches.

CONTEST ELEMENTS
The "rule-bound" aspects of the speech or debate.
Includes meeting contest rules and time limits.

to the competitive process. The contest dimensions include the special criteria of a competitive speech—adherence of the speaker to the contest rules and time limits.

While not as important as the substantive elements, the judge must carefully evaluate the contest issues in the debate. These elements exist for two reasons: to ensure fair competition and to define educational standards for the competition. They ensure fairness by making each competitor adhere to the same rules and they define the educational standards for the context by establishing criteria that the speakers must meet.

Contest rules are not uniform. Each tournament may have unique time limits or event descriptions. The judge has the obligation to follow and enforce those contest rules even if she does not agree with them. A judge may not obey some rules and ignore others. This undermines the integrity of the contest and the educational viability of the tournament. While teachers ought to be flexible, the contest judge, like a sports referee, cannot be flexible. Any failure to enforce a tournament rule, no matter what rationale is used, will inevitably be perceived as favoritism for or against another contestant.

The second facilitation activities include awarding points and writing constructive comments on ballots. Most contest situations require the judge to rank and rate speakers using both *nominal* and *ordinal* means.

The judge ranks speakers nominally in individual events, usually from 1 to 4. The judge gives a nominal ranking in debate rounds by deciding which team won. Both individual events and debate judges also give speaker ratings, which are ordinal numbers. The judge often has a wide range of points she can award. For instance, a typical debate ballot asks the judge to rate each speaker between 1 and 30. Many individual events ballots use a similar rating system.

The difficulty with ordinal data, of course, is its greater subjectivity. The contest judge must develop a rating system that is consistent from round to round. He should not, for example, give a speaker 25 rating points in one round, and a speaker that is generally the same in quality of performance 12 points in the next round. In this sense, rating points are much like classroom grades—teachers are expected to be both fair and consistent.

There is no universal formula for assigning rating points. The judge ought, however, to think about the criteria he employs in assigning points and attempt to be as systematic as possible. The appendix at the end of this chapter gives an example of a method developed by Diane Ritzdorf, a high school forensics teacher, for assigning speaker points in debate. Any judge could use this system or a similar one to develop his own means of systematically awarding points.

Ballot writing is the venue for the judge to both critique performance and explain the reasons for the competitive outcome. Both functions are very important. The ballot is not only an educational tool for student and teacher, but an explanation for competitive placing. Students need to know not only how they can improve but why they received a particular ranking or decision.

Some judges, particularly inexperienced ones, focus on one or the other of these functions. They may use the entire individual events ballot to critique the students speaking style or the entire debate ballot to justify the decision. While there is no rule prohibiting this approach, it does not make the most optimal use of the educational opportunity presented by the contest round. There are some guidelines for critiquing performance and explaining competitive rankings. First, the comments should be descriptive and not evaluative in tone. Second, the comments should address mechanical instead of pedagogical issues. Third, the comments should be provisional and not absolute. We will discuss these suggestions in the next section of this chapter.

The final aspect of facilitation is helping the tournament to run smoothly. Tournaments typically are tightly scheduled to include as many rounds as possible and to make the best use of facilities and judges. Judges will often listen to several consecutive rounds. The judge must help keep the tournament on time. She can do this by picking up her ballots on time, volunteering to judge extra rounds to help keep the tournament from falling behind, and by returning her ballots promptly.

These obligations are sometimes incompatible with other responsibilities. The judge may wish to visit with students or to take a few extra minutes writing a ballot. While these urges are important, they must be balanced with the need to keep the tournament running smoothly. Delays caused by one person have a ripple effect on the tournament, and all the competitors in a delayed round will be late for their next round. Another round cannot start in a competition room until the previous contestants have left.

The Judge as Trustee

The third and final function of the judge is as a trustee of the forensic activity. This function is, in a sense, the combination of both the roles of educator and facilitator. But this role is not simply confined to those activities. The judge is also the ultimate arbiter of the standards of the activity and the enforcer of ethical standards.

Forensics consists of both rule-bound and normative behaviors, a point discussed before. In many ways the norms are more significant than the rules, both in number and influence on the activity. The judge monitors students' normative behavior in forensics.

There are many examples of normative behaviors that the judge can influence; dress, deportment, language choices, acceptable kinds of evidence, and claims are a few examples. Judges can, for example, insist that competitors wear appropriate clothing, such as ties for men. Or they can require debaters or speakers to read complete source citations when giving their speeches. Students generally try to adapt to the judge if it is within their ability. Assuming the judge does not impose unreasonable demands, the student will comply.

The judge must be realistic in enforcing norms. First, she must be consistent and fair. The judge cannot use a norm in one context and not another, and cannot impose norms that are beyond the students' ability to meet. The judge should not knowingly impose norms that contradict the philosophy of another program or place students in the position of having to compromise their own beliefs or teachings to meet a judge's normative expectation.

Second, the norms must be educationally grounded. The judge should not impose whimsical norms that cannot be satisfactorily explained. For example, insisting that students tell jokes in their speeches may be purely whimsical and unrelated to the educational contest purpose. Judges should justify norms they use and explain them when students or teachers ask about them. This does not mean that others should attempt to refute these beliefs. All forensics participants must be open-minded enough to accept a wide variety of appropriate norms for competitive rounds.

Third, the student should have advance notice of the judges' preferences. Imposing norms places the burden on the judges to inform the competitors about their preferences and the reasons for imposing the norms. Judges should not impose a norm until students have the opportunity to consider the norm and ways of meeting it. This is especially true if the contestant is unfamiliar with a judge.

Giving advance notice of judging standards may not, however, be feasible in every circumstance. It is difficult, for example, for individual events judges to discuss their standards before a particular round. Students may not all be present at the beginning of the round. Similarly, inexperienced hired judges may not be comfortable in expressing their views. There are also experienced critics who prefer not to discuss their philosophies. They prefer the traditional view of the contest round as a place where the listener reacts to student presentations rather than attempting to shape the nature of the round through interaction.

The judge also is a trustee for the activity in enforcing high ethical standards. Chapter 9 will detail the kinds of ethical obligations followed in the activity. Generally, we expect the judge to enforce ethical standards based on fairness and honesty. This is similar to the duty of a classroom teacher to enforce similar standards, such as these connected with plagiarism.

PRACTICAL CONSIDERATIONS OF JUDGING FORENSICS EVENTS

Judging is not an easy task. It requires considerable concentration in a context where there is not much adrenaline flowing and where the judge also must think about other obligations as teacher and program director. Many rounds consist of flawed performances, which also makes listening difficult. In examining the practical considerations of judging several topics are found. This section considers skills needed for judging and how teachers and students can use judging comments to improve their performance.

Skills Needed for Judging

The judge must be a critical listener, an empathetic observer, and an accurate reporter of the competitive performances in the contest round.

The first necessary skill is for the judge to be a critical listener. The judge must pay close attention to the speech or debate and avoid some common listening difficulties that inhibit communicators.[1] The judge must avoid the temptation to focus solely on delivery instead of listening for content. This is sometimes difficult considering the fact that the judge will often listen to beginning speakers whose speaking skills lack polish. A judge inexperienced at judging debates may also focus on the rapid delivery of the speakers rather than attending closely to the content of the speeches. While delivery is important, it must be balanced with analyzing the speakers' content.

A judge also must be an empathetic observer. Empathy is, of course, desirable in all contexts. Empathy describes the ability to understand the feelings and behaviors of another person within a particular context. The empathetic person is able to understand behavior by recalling similar circumstances that he experienced. It is a particularly important characteristic of a contest speaking judge.

Contest speaking is occasionally both difficult and stressful. Success requires mastery of complicated skills and ideas. The competitive situation itself adds additional stress. The kinds of students who participate in forensics choose the activity partially because they are motivated to try hard to achieve success. They place much pressure on themselves to perform well, even before their skill level or knowledge catches up with their aspirations. Mastering forensics skills is gradual and marked by frequent stumbling blocks and plateaus. The nature of competition sometimes creates mismatches where a strong competitor or team is matched against an inferior one. All these elements combine to create a context where empathetic listening is very important.

A judge shows empathy both in his actions in the round and in his ballot comments. The judge must always behave respectfully toward the contestants. Creating a supportive climate through pleasant facial expressions and other extra-verbal expressions will help show empathy and respect for the students. The judge also should be careful not to be overly negative in comments he makes to the speakers after the round. Above all, the judge should be careful not to gossip about the round in the presence of others. Such comments often get back to the student and demonstrate a lack of empathy.

Empathy is also shown through the kinds of comments written on ballots. The previous section, in discussing the role of judge as facilitator, outlined three ideals in ballot writing. Those ideals are developed briefly here.

1. *The judge should be descriptive and not evaluative in tone when writing ballots.*

The judge should describe what happened in the round instead of making judgments about the value of those actions. For example, the judge might write "the first affirmative dropped the disadvantage and this lost the debate" instead of "the first affirmative dropped the disadvantage and this lost the debate. This person is clearly unable to debate at this level."

The judge should not usurp the role of the teacher by attempting to make coaching decisions. The judge also should not attempt to assign motives to behavior. For example, the judge should not punish a competitor on the ballot for not slavishly following the judges oral judging philosophy. The judge may describe what the competitor did, but should avoid evaluating the relative wisdom of the strategy.

2. *The comments should address mechanical and not pedagogical issues.*

As noted before, the judge is a secondary rather than primary teacher. The major responsibility for teaching strategy and techniques rests with the students' primary teacher. The judge should confine her observations to the actions in the contest round as opposed to discussing elements of pedagogical philosophy. The ballot, for instance, should not be used by the judge to express her feelings about the educational value of a forensics event, or her dislike for a debate-case area or an author of an interpretation selection.

The judge, in this respect, is more like a reporter than an editorial columnist. The reporter is bound by normal conventions of objectivity, meaning she should be neutral and even-handed. The editorial columnist is free to give her opinions regarding the meaning of events.

3. *The comments should be provisional rather than absolute in tone.*

The rationale for this suggestion is probably plain. There is a natural tendency for judges to use the ballot to issue absolute decrees about improvements that the speakers should make. Comments such as "you must change the topic of your persuasive speech," or "I will never vote for this case" are absolute in tone and largely inappropriate. The judge is entitled to dislike strategies or topics, but ought to state those beliefs provisionally.

A debate or individual events round is only a snapshot of a student's speaking and analytical abilities. A student may do something in a particular round that he would not do in another time. A competitive round is, of course, part of a system. A student's behavior may be influenced by other competitors, the perceived relationship with the judge, or a variety of other components that the judge cannot account for.

Students also react negatively to absolutist statements. They may feel alienated from the judge and resist making suggested changes in reaction to the perception that the judge is simply being excessively controlling.

4. *The judge should be an accurate reporter.*

As proved, a better model for judging is reporting rather than offering editorial commentary. The ballot is likely to be the only objective source of information about the competitive round. Competitors' perceptions will be colored by their biases about their performance and the competition. The ratings and rankings, while useful for the competitive operation of the tournament, do not tell much about the round. It is only the judge's ballot that can help the students learn how to improve or give them information about why they won or lost.

Another important justification for good reporting skills is the importance of the ballot as a source of teaching. As you will see shortly, using the ballots as a teaching tool is extremely important. The teacher will be using the ballot to look for patterns of behavior that show how the student is speaking and what could be changed. Being able to rely on a judge for consistent, helpful, and accurate comments is a great help to the teacher.

Accurate reporting involves several skills. First, the judge should have a sound ballot writing philosophy, including understanding the audience, context, and philosophy. The audience is, of course, not only the competitor but also the judge. Situation specific comments about a round are not as helpful to the judge as more general comments about the arguing and speaking skills. Situation specific comments are important as the means of explaining a decision, but they must be balanced against general comments. Context is also important. Any suggestions or observations should be explained. The student and the teacher need information about the judge to understand her point of view. The judge also must have a philosophy about writing a ballot. This involves being systematic in observing the round and writing the ballot.

Second, the judge needs to be skilled in concentration and be willing to take the necessary time to write effectively. As noted previously, judges are often overworked and have competing priorities. Not every round is intellectually engaging. Despite these very real problems, judges will be expected to give their total attention to the round and to take the necessary time to write a useful ballot. The judge cannot linger excessively over a ballot or it may make the tournament run off schedule. This suggests that the judge must prioritize her comments and not make every suggestion as though she has unlimited time and space.

Third, the judge should be able to elaborate rather than truncate. Judges sometimes write comments in code. They abbreviate a lot ("dropped turn / 2B = no h") and do not explain their comments. Instead, a good ballot explains comments fully, takes the time to justify assertions, and describes both the positive and negative elements of the presentation.

Fourth, though it may seem trivial, a judge must have good handwriting. Even the most helpful comments will go unheeded if they cannot be read. Concentration and effort should help even the person with poor handwriting to write clearly enough to be understood.

How Students and Teachers Use Ballots

Ballots are a critical educational tool for forensics teachers. To a large extent, forensics education is post facto. While all the pre-tournament learning activities (such as practice rounds, brainstorming meetings, and analysis sessions) are important, they cannot completely prepare students for the realities of actual competition.

Competition is the chance students have to test their skills and identify their weaknesses. The systemic nature of forensics competition guarantees a healthy mixture of success and failure. Students will learn what they are doing well and what others do better. In a healthy educational environment, the student comes home from the tournament excited about his success and aware of ways he can improve. The teacher can channel that enthusiasm in productive ways, suggesting specific strategies for remedying weaknesses and building on strengths.

The teacher must depend largely on ballots to help her devise strategies for helping students improve. The ballots are the data that the teacher uses to learn trends and tendencies of students. In using ballots, the teacher must keep several considerations in mind.

1. *No particular ballot is necessarily significant.* A teacher or competitor cannot always focus on the comments of a single ballot and consider them indicative of skill or knowledge. Occasionally, individual ballots will be particularly helpful, especially if the teacher and competitor know the judge or the ballot is consistent with how the teacher observed the round. For the most part, however, a particular round is idiosyncratic. Human behavior is best understood through repetition. Skills are best revealed over time and accumulation of comments. Students and teachers should give greater weight to comments appearing in several ballots than ones that appear only once.

2. *The skill and expertise of the judge in evaluating comments is only of partial importance.* There is a natural tendency to assign greater credibility to judges who have a reputation as a good judge or for their own competitive success. Noted earlier, a particular round is not a good measure of the expertise of a competitor. The same generalization holds true for judges. No judge can operate at peak efficiency in every round. There will be rounds where the judge is distracted and unable to focus as much attention on the round or the ballot as she would like. Similarly, good teachers do not necessarily make good judges. There are differences between being a competitively successful forensics teacher and a good judge — the ability at one does not guarantee the ability at the other.

3. *The competitive ballot is a poor communication instrument.* While difficult to quantify, common sense tells us that not everything that happens in a competitive round will be reported accurately on a ballot. At the most general level, eyewitness testimony is often unreliable. People may see the same event in entirely different ways. In terms of the specifics of a forensics contest, judges may be influenced by factors that they are unable or unwilling to report on the ballot.

A judge may, for instance, have a negative impression of a speaker's clothing or haircut. Since that would be inappropriate to use as a factor in a decision, the judge finds another acceptable criterion to explain the negative decision. Similarly, the judge may be reluctant to offend another teacher, who also could be a judge, by being entirely candid about the round. Judging, like many other human communication contexts, is political behavior.

4. *The judge may not be an effective written communicator.* Little attention is given in forensics to written communication. Since the main focus is oral communication, the typical judge probably is more comfortable in speaking than in writing. Law students spend a great deal of time learning to write, but there is usually no training for forensics contest judges, and if training happens, little or no time is spent on writing skills.

The preceding discussion should not be interpreted as a negative commentary toward judges. I suspect that a similar indictment could be made of legal opinions or other forms of written reasoning. Our appellate system is based on the fact that one of the parties in a dispute remains unconvinced by the reasoning the judge used to settle a dispute. The profession of contract law thrives because people cannot express themselves accurately in their written contracts. The ballot is the only usable tool to describe the events in a forensics contest. For better or worse, it is the tool that teachers must rely on.

There are some specific ways in which teachers can use contest ballots. They can do *content analysis*; they can use the ballots as discussion tools or as *motivational means*.[2]

Content Analysis

Content analysis is a useful way to systematize reading ballots and using comments. Content analysis involves extracting units of data from a document and deciding the significance of those extracted units.[3] While many scholars use sophisticated content analysis techniques, complexity is not required for using this tool.

The teacher could use simple content analysis to examine judges' comments about speaking or analytical variables. For example, they could focus specifically on comments related to "organization" in extemporaneous or impromptu speaking. Or they might look for missing comments, because the lack of a particular comment in several ballots may be important. For example, if judges never comment about disadvantages that a negative team is stressing, perhaps that shows that these arguments against are not very important for debates and should be changed.

The content analysis process also does not need to be extensive. One technique is to save ballots in individual notebooks for each student or team. Then the teacher can use a highlighter to mark individual comments to be used to discuss with the student or to prepare teaching strategies.

Discussion Tool

The second use of ballots is for discussing performance with the student. After the tournament, the teacher can schedule a time to debrief the student about his performance, using comments from ballots as a discussion agenda. The teacher should usually choose one or two areas to work on at a time, then perhaps use comments on the ballots from the next tournament to see if there are changes in the particular behavior.

Motivation

Third, the teacher can use the ballots to motivate the student. In this instance, the teacher should look for both positive and negative comments and emphasize positive ones as evidence of improvement and negative ones as a prod for improvement. The teacher also could use the comments to encourage the student to work on her adaptation to a particular judge who may have a negative impression of the student. Impressing that particular judge may become a goal for a future tournament.

SUMMARY

This chapter discusses the philosophy and practice of judging. Judging is a critical element of forensics education, as judges will often observe more about student performance than the student's own teacher. The judge has three roles: educator, facilitator, and trustee of the activity. Also examined were some practical considerations of forensics judging, and the skills necessary to effectively judge, along with some ways that teachers and students can use ballot comments for improvement. The appendix gives an example of a rubric for awarding speaker points in debate rounds and an article discussing judging standards for oral interpretation contests.

The last three chapters have examined the educational systems of forensics, including teaching and learning debate, individual events, and judging forensics contests. The final chapters of the book, which conclude Part II, examine two additional topic areas—learning resources for the forensics teacher and the ethics of forensics education.

ACTIVITIES

1. Discuss your educational philosophy of judging contest rounds. How is it the same or different from your philosophy of critiquing classroom speaking performance?

2. Examine some contest ballots written for students at your school. What distinguishes good from poor ballots? What kinds of comments would be particularly helpful to a teacher or a contestant?

3. If possible, photocopy some ballots you write while at a tournament. Have another class member critique your ballots and offer suggestions on how they might be improved.

NOTES

1. Lyman K. Steil, Larry Barker, and Kitty Watson, *Effective Listening*. (Reading: Addison-Wesley, 1983).

2. An excellent discussion of using ballots to improve individual events performance is found in Mary Ann Renz, "Strategies for Increasing the Use of Ballots in Coaching Individual Events." *National Forensic Journal*, 9 (1991): 167–172. See also C. T. Hanson, "What Are the Options: The Philosophy of Using Ballots." *The Forensic of Pi Kappa Delta*, 74 (1988): 1–6.

3. Kristine M. Bartanen, "Use of Criteria Referenced Ballots for Individual Events." *National Forensic Journal*, 8 (1991): 133–144.

APPENDIX TO CHAPTER 7

The following article was written by Diane Ritzdorf and published in the *Speech Communication Teacher*, Fall 1988, pp. 10–11.

Awarding Speaker Points in Cross-Examination Debate

Goal: To provide a more objective way of awarding speaker points in cross-examination debate.

I developed this rubric when I realized that the 30 high school students in my 2-hour-a-week debate class would have very few opportunities to participate in a full scale debate if I, as the teacher, had to listen to every debate and grade every debater. I wanted some way to employ students as critics, as well as provide a grade for the student debaters. This would allow several debates to occur simultaneously in different classrooms with student judges evaluating each one.

I use the Colorado High School Activities Association CX debate ballot that provides a grid for awarding speaker points to each speaker, based on 7 criteria: analysis, reasoning, evidence, organization, refutation, ethics, and delivery. After defining each criterion, I indicate what observable behaviors merit a score of 5, 4, or 3 in that area. I concentrate on the upper end of the point scale because I want the student judges to reward honest efforts by novice debaters positively. Only very minimal efforts deserve low speaker points. You can find the form for evaluating a CX debate on page 136.

Before in-class debate rounds begin, I spend one or more class sessions instructing students in the use of the rubric and completing the ballot. This includes providing examples of good and poor debate techniques and watching and evaluating a videotaped debate. I encourage students to explain speaker points in their comments to each individual speaker.

When scheduling in-class debates, I also assign 3 or 4 students to serve as judges for each debate. After the debate, a copy of each completed ballot is given to the affirmative and negative team, as well as to me. I average the points awarded by each judge for each student to determine each

EVALUATING A CX DEBATE

A Rubric		Name	

Directions: Use the following criteria, discussed in class, to award speaker points in the debates that you evaluate. Remember, the winning team should receive the most speaker points.

POINTS:	5	4	3
ANALYSIS	Examines stock issues AND other side's arguments	Examines stock issues OR other side's arguments	Examines only superficial issues; no depth
REASONING	Explains each argument/ evidence in logical way	Explains arguments and evidence part of the time	Reads evidence without explaining it; 1 or 2 arguments don't make sense
EVIDENCE	Factual information to support all major arguments	Some facts that support some of the points	Evidence not directly related; mostly general quotes and opinions
ORGANIZATION	Maintains organization throughout constructive and rebuttal speeches	Only constructive speech is organized	Only part of constructive speech is organized
REPUTATION	Answers arguments directly; extends	Answers directly; repeats	Does not answer directly; repeats
ETHICS	No infractions of the rules; courteous	No major infractions; some discourtesies	One major infraction; discourtesies
DELIVERY	Fluent; persuasive; eye contact; comfortable rate	Problem with one area	Problem with two areas

debater's grade and to evaluate the student judge, based on how well his/her ballot explains the speaker points and reason for decision. I have used this rubric for several years. The results have been positive. All students get more experience as debaters. They get feedback from a greater number of critics and have a more objective method of interpreting those ballots. The student judges learn how to debate, through critical listening, and have some actual judging experience before they become critics at novice tournaments.

In the fall of 1987, the Colorado Speech Critic Certification Committee distributed the rubric at critic training clinics. Beginning critics felt more confident with the guidelines, and experienced critics commented that it helped them award points more consistently.

8
Learning Resources in Forensics

CHAPTER OVERVIEW

This chapter discusses various places where a teacher can go to discover more information about topics connected with forensics. It gives an overview of the history of forensics research and provides a helpful bibliography.

Like any discipline, forensics has many resources that both new or experienced teachers can use to improve their knowledge and teaching skills. These include standard printed references like textbooks and journal articles, specialized resources like handbooks, and interpersonal or group resources (as in peer assistance and workshops). This chapter discusses some of these resources, with the purpose of providing a starting point for finding helpful information.

Most of the material in this text is up-to-date and probably will remain so for a while. This won't be the case for this chapter, however. We confront, as inhabitants of an information-based society, an exploding information base. Twenty years ago, for example, a bibliography of forensics would be considerably shorter. The list of resources was sufficiently manageable for educators to stay current in the field. This is no longer the case. The growing importance of computer technology has greatly expanded the ability of people to access increasing amounts of information easily. I can, for example, access a university computer from my own home via computer modem, which allows me to collect more information on a given topic in a few hours than I could in months of research writing a doctoral dissertation fifteen years ago!

This means that the information found here should be considered simply a starting point for further research in forensics education. Like any discipline, forensics is always growing and evolving, and you will encounter new resources constantly. Unlike other disciplines, forensics is still immature in its theory and research.[1] Forensics theory did not begin to show real growth until the 1960s. Prior to that time, there was little theoretical development of debate or individual events. A few major textbooks dominated debate theory and there was virtually no individual events theory independent of public speaking training and research.

AN OVERVIEW OF RESEARCH IN DEBATE AND INDIVIDUAL EVENTS

The 1960s saw a rapid growth in debate theory. Introduction of general systems theory to debate, leading to use of comparative advantages and other innovations, fueled increasing interest in debate theory. The content of articles and books began to concentrate more on various debate theory questions. Highly influential textbook authors introduced the first editions of their books, updating debate theory and generating research in debate scholarship. Austin Freeley,[2] Douglas Ehninger and Wayne Brockriede,[3] and Glen Mills,[4] were authors of three of these important textbooks. Interest in argumentation theory paralleled the growth in debate theory.

Stephen Toulmin's 1958 book *The Uses of Argument* and Chaim Perelman's 1969 book *The New Rhetoric* (originally published in French and later translated into English) represented new directions in argumentation theory that diverged sharply from debate theory.[5] Toulmin's model of argument, in particular, became highly influential and textbook authors adopted it as a theoretical tool for describing an argument. The Toulmin model, in its simplified form, is widely known:

Toulmin's model, as part of a broader theory grounding argumentation in "fields" as opposed to "formal logic," radically changed forensics theory.[6] Debate theory began to apply organizational theory and political science precepts to the practice of debate. Gradual acceptance of debate and individual events fields encouraged much more theoretical and practical research.

The 1970s brought increasing interest in two new areas—individual events and nonpolicy debate. As discussed in Chapter 1, these events emerged as important educational and competitive forces during this time. Introduction of the National Forensic Association national individual events championship (later emulated by the American Forensic Association championship) and the Cross-Examination Debate Association as an alternative to college policy debate created new opportunities for research.

Interest in individual events and nonpolicy debate also grew in high school competition. Unfortunately, there are fewer research opportunities or studies of high school activities. High school programs derive most of their theory from research conducted at the college level. This is a result of the fact that college teachers are encouraged and occasionally rewarded for conducting research, while high school teachers are not. This has inevitably led to a gap between theory and practice at the high school level. Integration of new theoretical perspectives at the high school level has been uneven. Debate theory, in particular, is increasingly disseminated to high school students through high school debate institutes, bypassing the teacher almost completely. There are several magazines and journals that provide articles aimed at discussing high school debate theory. *The Rostrom* and *Debate Issues*[7] are two prominent examples.

Research in individual events theory emerged primarily through publication of proceedings of summer conferences on individual events and articles in journals.[8] The research is primarily descriptive in nature. The research began to sketch the nature of competitive public speaking and its differences from other public speaking contexts. Other articles described the nature of forensic events and techniques for successful competition.

Research in nonpolicy debate is found primarily in the *CEDA Yearbook*. This publication began modestly as an informally published collection of articles edited by Don Brownlee. The Cross-Examination Debate Association later expanded it into a yearly refereed publication.[9] Textbooks began including sections on nonpolicy debate or having nonpolicy debate as their major focus.[10]

Debate theory in recent years has separated from the larger argumentation field. Argumentation scholars have broadened their emphasis in areas such as argument fields and structure. Much of the research in academic debate has narrowed toward technical issues concerned with resolutional interpretation.[11]

Overall, forensics research has grown substantially in recent years. Early research had its place primarily in the mainstream communication journals and often concerned the benefits of debate or provided general suggestions for participating in forensic activities. More complete debate theories were developed beginning in the 1950s with the introduction of several influential textbooks. Journals such as *JAFA, The Rostrum,* and others sponsored by forensics fraternities gave increasing opportunities for articles on debate and individual events. This led to increasing specialization in forensics articles.

The next two sections introduce resources available to forensics educators. The first section surveys print resources, and the second examines workshops and seminars as resources.

PRINT RESOURCES IN FORENSICS

Print resources in forensics include four types: books, journal articles, printed convention papers, and debate handbooks.

Books on Debate Theory and Practice

There are many books on debate theory and practice and few on individual events. As noted earlier, the growth of forensics in the 1950s led to publication of several books for classroom use. Most major publishers began to carry argumentation and debate textbooks as part of their offerings in communication.

Textbooks today tend to be more specialized. The most often used debate textbook in college debate is Austin Freeley's.[12] This book began as a policy debate text and is still heavily oriented in that direction. There are chapters in more recent editions on college value debate. The book has stood the test of time as a clear and "user-friendly" introduction to policy debate. It is appropriate for use by both college and high school students and is highly useful for a teacher lacking background in argumentation and debate theory.

There is no corresponding text aimed exclusively at high school debate that is as useful as the Freeley textbook. For example, one of the more popular books, written by Roy Wood, is a clear introductory text without much theory or attention to other debate forms.[13]

There are several textbooks discussing team value debate for college students. Wood and Midgeley, Church and Willbanks, and Bartanen and Frank are commonly used books for beginning students. In Lincoln-Douglas debate, both the National Association of High School Activity Associations and the National Textbook Company publish textbooks teaching skills in Lincoln-Douglas.[14]

One type of textbook, the anthology, is particularly useful for debate teachers. A popular anthology is edited by David Thomas and John Hart. *Advanced Debate*, in its fourth edition, is a collection of reprinted and original articles on a wide range of debate theory topics.[15] The articles cover issues of debate practice and a wide range of theoretical issues connected to policy debate, value debate, and debate judging. As in any anthology, individual articles are uneven in quality and the reasons for selecting particular articles are not always clear. But the book remains a valuable resource for either high school or college students and teachers. *Advanced Debate* is part of a group of books published by the same publisher.[16]

Books on Individual Events Theory and Practice

While there are few books devoted exclusively to individual events, there are hundreds of public speaking and oral interpretation texts to choose from. The large number of high schools and colleges offering public speaking courses gives teachers many choices regarding books. The range of public speaking texts goes from very prescriptive texts to ones that are more theoretical.

Beginning students may prefer more prescriptive texts, such as ones by Sprague and Stuart and Littlefield.[17] These textbooks present specific steps the speaker can use to construct speeches. The Sprague and Stuart book has an excellent outline of speaking steps for students. Both textbooks discuss ideas like visual aids and supporting materials that are especially appropriate for inexperienced students.

There are other short books and pamphlets exclusively for individual events competition. While they give students an introduction to speaking techniques they do not give much holistic training in speaking.

Journal Articles on Forensics

Important sources of information on forensics are articles in professional journals and magazines. Like all professional disciplines, communication has many journals devoted to research on communication-related topics. Figure 8.1 lists journals that publish articles on forensics.

Argumentation and Advocacy, formerly the *Journal of the American Forensic Association*, is published by the American Forensic Association. The journal combines forensics articles with argumentation theory articles. The journal is indexed in the *Education Index*. The *NFA Journal, The Forensic of Pi Kappa Delta*, and *Speaker and Gavel* are all forensics related journals published by college forensics organizations. They contain articles about both debate and individual events. They are all generally refereed

FIGURE 8.1 Journals with articles on forensics.

Argument and Advocacy
NFA Journal
The Rostrum
Debate Issues
Communication Education
The Forensic of Pi Kappa Delta
Forensic Quarterly
The Speech Communication Teacher
Speaker and Gavel
CEDA Yearbook

journals, meaning that the articles have been blindly reviewed prior to being published. The difficulty with using these resources is that they are not externally indexed.[18]

The CEDA Yearbook is published annually by the Cross-Examination Debate Association and has articles primarily on college value debate. *The Rostrum* is the publication of the National Forensic League and contains some articles in addition to material on NFL activities.[19] Neither of these publications are generally indexed in library indexes.

Articles on forensics also appear in other communication journals on occasion. One useful journal for teachers is *Communication Education*. Published by the Speech Communication Association, this journal publishes articles related to teaching and learning issues in communication.[20] It has been recently supplemented by another publication, *The Speech Communication Teacher*. This publication is an excellent teaching resource for classroom speech teachers or forensics teachers. It contains many short articles providing innovative teaching methods. Several of the articles in that publication have supplemented this text.

Printed Convention Papers

There are conventions that occur regularly where people present papers on forensics issues. Often these papers are available in print. The Speech Communication Association convention is also the place where many forensics related associations, such as the AFA, NFA, and CEDA meet. There are many convention panels on forensics topics and often the papers at these panels are reprinted in the ERIC system.[21] This is also true of the regional communication association conventions (Western Speech Communication Association, Central States Speech Association, Eastern Communication Association, and the Southern Speech Association).

There are also other forensics conventions that publish collections of the presented papers. A Summer Argumentation Conference is held biennially at Alta, Utah. This conference has panels on argumentation and forensics, and its proceedings are published by the Speech Communication Association. There have also been summer conferences on CEDA Debate, Individual Events, and High School Activities, all of whom later published their proceedings.

Debate Handbooks

Debate handbooks have become increasingly popular in recent years. Besides supplying prepared evidence on a debate topic they often include articles on debate theory and analysis. Since these books are privately published, the articles are not refereed and depend on the knowledge of the authors, who are sometimes undergraduate college students. Handbooks should be used carefully, and used primarily for gathering debate evidence rather than as a source of debate theory.[22]

WORKSHOPS AND SEMINARS IN FORENSICS

Another source of information in forensics is found in workshops and seminars. There are many summer workshops for high school debaters and teachers each summer, and some for college debaters and teachers. Some workshops also include individual events teaching.

The National Association of High School Activities Association publishes a list of summer high school workshops, and many workshops use extensive mailing lists in an attempt to contact as many students as possible.

Workshops vary widely in their philosophy and organization. Some workshops are aimed primarily at experienced students, others at novices. Some rely heavily on group lectures and others on laboratory group experiences. Students and teachers ought to evaluate carefully a summer institute before attending. Like choosing a college, selecting a debate institute is an important decision that depends heavily on the interests and philosophy of the student and her program. Figure 8.2 lists some criteria that a student and teacher ought to consider in selecting a summer institute.

Summer institutes can be expensive to attend and vary considerably in their quality. Some institutes are aimed at "stars" or students who have shown talent and success. These institutes may prepare students for highly sophisticated debates and complex arguments and may not be appropriate for the beginning or intermediate student.

Other institutes are more local or regional in philosophy. They may stress basic skills and give opportunities to participate in individual events. There are also resident institutes and commuter institutes. At resident institutes, students stay on campus during the institute and are supervised and chaperoned by institute staff. This can give a taste of college life. Commuter institutes (where students return home at the end of the day),

FIGURE 8.2 Some criteria for selecting a summer institute.

1. What will the educational experience be like? Will it include lecture, small group activities, library work, and actual practice?

2. Who is the faculty? Does it include college teachers who are active forensics educators? Successful college debaters? Experienced and effective high school teachers? Will each student get to work with all the faculty?

3. What is the learning environment? Is the institute held on a college campus? Will students be able to use the library? Will the students always be chaperoned?

while often less expensive, may trade off the cost savings if students do not work as hard as they might if they were at a resident institute.

The educational value of summer institutes is a question of some interest. There is no empirical data on whether these institutes help or hinder learning forensics skills. They are likely valuable in helping students in programs where the students do not have access to library resources during the debate season. This may give students the chance to learn about college life and how to use a college library. An institute also may expose students to debate theories that may be used in tournaments during the year.

Debate institutes, however, also have some disadvantages. An institute that is not philosophically compatible with the high school program may cause dissonance and conflict between the teacher and students. The student may develop skills (like rapid delivery) with which the teacher is uncomfortable. Careful selection of an institute with regard to the institute's philosophy and educational practices is important to avoiding these kinds of problems.

There are also summer workshops for teachers. While not as many as ones for students, many colleges have workshops to teach new and experienced teachers and provide college credit. These workshops are often advertised along with student workshops.

A BIBLIOGRAPHY OF FORENSICS

The final section of this chapter consists of a bibliography of some resources available in forensics. It is not meant as a comprehensive bibliography, but simply as a starting point to locate resources that can prove helpful in teaching forensics activities. It does not include all the sources used in other sections of this text, but is a sampling of the kinds of issues forensics educators are writing and thinking about. Many of these articles are examples of scholarly discussions in the discipline. You should not assume that these articles are necessarily the best or the only articles on these subjects. (Note: The bibliography is organized by subject heading.)

Conference Proceedings

Cox, J. Robert, et al., eds., *Argument and Social Practice: Proceedings of the Speech Communication Association/American Forensic Association Conference on Argumentation, (Alta, Ut. 1984).* (Annandale: American Forensic Assoc. and SCA, 1985).

McBath, J. H., ed., *Forensics as Communication: The Argumentative Perspective.* (Skokie: National Textbook, 1975.)

Parson, D. W., ed., *American Forensics in Perspective: Papers from the National Conference on Forensics (Evanston, Illinois, September 12–15, 1984)*. (Annandale: SCA, 1984).

Rhodes, J. and S. Newell, eds., *Proceedings of the Summer Conference on Argumentation (Alta, Ut. July 26–29, 1979)*. (Falls Church: SCA, 1980).

Thomas, D. and S. Wood, eds., *CEDA 1991: 20th Anniversary Assessment Conference Proceedings*, (St. Paul, MN, August 13–15, 1991). (Dubuque: Kendall-Hunt, 1993).

Zarefsky, D., et. al., *Argument in Transition: Proceedings of the Summer Conference on Argumentation (Alta, Ut. July 28–31, 1983)*. (Annandale: SCA, 1983).

Ziegelmueller, G. and J. Rhodes, eds., *Dimensions of Argument: Proceedings of the Summer Conference on Argumentation (Alta, Ut. July 30–August 2, 1981)*. (Annandale: SCA, 1981).

Debate Theory—Anthology of Articles

Thomas, D. and J. Hart, *Advanced Debate: Readings in Theory, Practice, and Teaching*, 4th edition. (Chicago: National Textbook, 1992).

Ethics of Forensics

Frank, R. L. "The Abuse of Evidence in Persuasive Speaking." *National Forensic Journal*, 1 (1983): 97–107.

Thomas, D. A. "The Ethics of Speech Events: A Survey of Standards Used by Contestants and Judges." *National Forensic Journal*, 1 (1983): 1–17.

Towne, R. "Rat-A-Tat-Tat—A Symposium on Humanizing Forensics," *Speaker and Gavel*, 12 (1974): 8–10.

Educational Value of Forensics

Colbert, K., "The Effects of CEDA and NDT Debate Training on Critical Thinking Ability." *Journal of the American Forensic Association*, 23 (1987): 194–201.

Colbert, K., and T. Biggers, "Why Should We Support Debate?" *Journal of the American Forensic Association*, 21 (1985): 237–240.

Hill, B., "Intercollegiate Debate: Why Do Students Bother?" *Southern Speech Communication Journal,* 48 (1982): 77–88.

McGough, M., "Pull it Across Your Flow." *The New Republic,* 199 (1988): 17–19.

McGucken, H., "Better Forensics—An Impossible Dream?" *Journal of the American Forensic Association.* 8 (1972): 182–185.

Pearce, W. B., "Attitudes Toward Forensics." *Journal of the American Forensic Association.* 10 (1974): 134–139.

Rowland, R. C. and S. Deatherage, "The Crisis in Policy Debate." *Journal of the American Forensic Association,* 24 (1988): 246–250.

Thomas, D. A., "Forensics Shock: Making Forensics Relevant to Tomorrow's Higher Education." *Speech Teacher,* 23 (1974): 235–241.

Ziegelmueller, G., "Policy Debate: A Retrospective and Prospective View." *Argumentation and Advocacy.* 27 (1990): 26–30.

Individual Events Theory and Practice

Benoit, W. L. and M. D. Moeder, *The Theory of Rhetorical Criticism: A Bibliography.* (Annandale: Speech Communication Assoc., 1989).

Benson, J. A. "Extemporaneous Speaking: Organization Which Inheres." *Journal of the American Forensic Association,* 14 (1978): 150–155.

Benson, J. A. and S. A. Friedley, "An Empirical Analysis of Evaluation Criteria for Public Speaking." *Journal of the American Forensic Association,* 19 (1982): 1–13.

Bytwerk, R. L. "Impromptu Speaking Exercises." *Communication Education,* 34 (1985): 148–49.

Crawford, J. E. "Toward Standardized Extemporaneous Speech Competition: Tournament Design and Speech Training. *National Forensic Journal,* 2 (1984): 41–55.

Dean, K. W., "Time Well Spent: Preparation for Impromptu Speaking." *Journal of the American Forensic Association,* 23 (1987): 210–219.

Dean, K. W. and W. L. Benoit, "A Categorical Content Analysis of Rhetorical Criticism Ballots." *National Forensic Journal,* 2 (1984): 99–108.

Lee, C. I., *Oral Interpretation, 6th ed.* (Boston: Houghton-Mifflin, 1988).

Lewis, T. V. et. al., "Evaluating Oral Interpretation Events: A Contest and Festival Perspectives Symposium." *National Forensic Journal,* 2 (1984): 19–32.

Mohrmann, G. P. and S. J. Kaplan, "The Effect of Training on the Oral Interpreter's Perception of a Text." *Central States Speech Journal,* 31 (1980): 137–142.

Pelias, R. J., "Evaluating Interpretation Events on the Forensic Circuit." *Journal of the American Forensic Association,* 20 (1984): 224–230.

Pelias, R. J., "Oral Interpretation as a Training Method for Perspective-Taking Abilities." *Communication Education,* 33 (1984): 143–151.

Schrier, W., *Contest Oratory: A Handbook for High School and College Contestants and Coaches.* (Menchen, NJ: Scarecrow, 1971).

Van Metre, P. D., "Oral Interpretation: A Path to Meaning." *Language Arts,* 54 (1977): 278–282.

Witter-Merithew, A., *Curriculum Guide for the Instruction of Oral Interpreting.* (Alexander Graham, 1985).

Work, W., "A Matter of Interpretation: ERIC Report." *Communication Education,* 32 (1983): 349–355.

Judging and Judging Paradigms

Balthrop, V. W., "A Debate Judge as 'Critic of Argument': Toward A Transcendent Perspective." *Journal of the American Forensic Association,* 20 (1983): 1–15.

Brey, J., "A Descriptive Analysis of CEDA Judging Philosophies Part I: Definitive Acceptance or Rejection of Certain Tactics and Arguments." *CEDA Yearbook,* 10 (1989): 67–77.

Littlefield, R. S., *Judging Oral Interpretation Events.* (Kansas City: National Federation of State High School Assoc., 1987.)

Rowland, R. C., "Special Forum: Debate Paradigms I. Standards for Paradigm Evaluation." *Journal of the American Forensic Association,* 18 (1982): 133–140.

Rowland, R. C., "The Debate Judge as Debate Judge: A Functional Paradigm for Evaluating Debates." *Journal of the American Forensic Association,* 20 (1984): 183–193.

Rowland, R. C., *"Tabula Rasa:* The Relevance of Debate to Argumentation Theory." *Journal of the American Forensic Association,* 21 (1984): 76–88.

Ulrich, W., "Debate as Dialectic: A Defense of the *Tabula Rasa* Approach to Judging." *Journal of the American Forensic Association,* 21 (1984): 89–93.

Ulrich, W., *Guidelines for the Debate Judge.* (Kansas City: National Federation of State High School Assns., 1988).

Zarefsky, D., "Reflections on Hypothesis Testing in Response to Ulrich." *Journal of the American Forensic Association*, 21 (1984): 9–13.

Lincoln-Douglas Debate

Bartanen, M. and D. Frank, *Lincoln-Douglas Debate: Preparing for Value Argumentation,* (Lincolnwood: National Textbook Co., 1993).

Mezzera, D. and G. Giertz, *Student Congress and Lincoln-Douglas Debate,* 2nd ed. (Lincolnwood: National Textbook, 1989).

Thomas, D., *Lincoln-Douglas Debate.* (Kansas City: National Federation of State High School Assns., 1981).

Thomas, D. and M. Fryar, *Student Congress and Lincoln-Douglas Debate.* (Skokie: National Textbook, 1981).

Policy Debate Theory

Lichtman, R. J. and D. M. Rohrer, "A General Theory of the Counterplan. *Journal of the American Forensic Association,* 12 (1975): 70–79.

Madsen, A. and A. Louden, "The Jurisdiction/Topicality Analogy." *Argumentation and Advocacy,* 26 (1990): 151–154.

Morello, J. T. and R. A. Soenksen, "Debate Rules and the Future of Policy Debate." *Argumentation and Advocacy,* 26 (1989): 11–21.

Paulsen, J. W. and J. Rhodes, "The Counter-Warrant as Negative Strategy: A Modest Proposal." *Journal of the American Forensic Association,* 15 (1979): 205–210.

Perkins, D. A., "Counterplans and Paradigms." *Argumentation and Advocacy,* 25 (1989): 140–149.

Solt, R., "Negative Fiat: Resolving the Ambiguities of 'Should.' " *Argumentation and Advocacy,* 25 (1989): 121–139.

Ulrich, W. R., "Counterplan Theory and the Power to Select Resolutions." *Argumentation and Advocacy,* 26 (1990): 154–159.

Program Administration and Justification

Ballard-Reich, D., "The Small College Director of Forensics." *Association for Communication Administration Bulletin,* 54 (1985): 76–78.

Faules, D. F., R. D. Rieke, and J. Rhodes, *Directing Forensics.* (Denver: Morton, 1978).

Prochaska, R. J., "Forensics Education at Public Junior and Community Colleges: A National Survey." *Journal of the American Forensic Association,* 18 (1981): 120–129.

Debate Practices

Alex, N. K., "Debate and Communication Skills." *ERIC Digest.* (Bloomington: ERIC Clearinghouse on Reading and Communication Skills, 1991).

Brown, P. M., *The Art of Questions: Thirty Maxims of Cross-Examination.* (New York: Macmillan, 1987).

Henderson, B., "A System of Teaching Cross-Examination Techniques." *Communication Education,* 27 (1978): 112–118.

Mayer, M. E. and V. D. Meldrum, "The Effect of Various Time Limits on the Quality of Rebuttals." *Journal of the American Forensic Association,* 23 (1987): 158–165.

Spiker, B.K., T. D. Daniels, and L. M. Bernabo, "The Quantitative Quandry in Forensics: The Use and Abuse of Statistical Evidence." *Journal of the American Forensic Association,* 19 (1982): 87–96.

Vasilius, J. M. and D. DeStephen, "An Investigation of the Relationship Between Debate Tournament Success and Rate, Evidence, and Jargon." *Journal of the American Forensic Association,* 15 (1979): 197–204.

Sample Debates and Speeches

Boaz, J. K. and J. R. Brey, eds., *Championship Debates and Speeches,* Volume 1. (Annandale: American Forensic Assoc. and Speech Communication Assoc., 1986).

National Forensic League, "Championship Final Rounds." audiotapes. (Ripon: National Forensic League).

Textbooks on Debate and Forensics

Bartanen, M. D. and D. A. Frank, *Debating Values.* (Scottsdale: Gorsuch Scarisbrick, 1990).

Church, R. T. and C. L. Wilbanks, *Values and Policies in Controversy: An Introduction to Argumentation and Debate,* 2nd ed. (Dubuque: Kendall-Hunt, 1991).

Freely, A. J., *Argumentation and Debate: Critical Thinking for Reasoned Decision-Making,* 6th ed. (New York: Wadsworth, 1990).

Fryar, M., D. Thomas, and L. Goodnight, *Basic Debate,* 3rd ed. (Lincolnwood: National Textbook, 1989).

Keefe, C., T. Harte, and L. Norton, *Introduction to Debate.* (New York: Macmillan, 1982).

Pfau, M. W., et al., *Debate and Argument: A Systems Approach to Advocacy.* (New York: Scott, Foresman, 1987).

Rieke, R. D., and M. O. Sillars, *Argumentation and the Decision-Making Process.* (New York: John Wiley and Sons, 1975).

Wood, R., *Strategic Debate,* 2nd ed. (Lincolnwood: National Textbook, 1977).

Wood, S. and J. Midgely, eds., *Prima Facie.* (Dubuque: Kendall-Hunt, 1986).

Wood, S. and J. B. Miller, *Debate Tournament Administration.* (Dubuque: Kendall-Hunt, 1988).

Textbooks on Public Speaking

DeVito J., *The Elements of Public Speaking,* 4th ed. (New York: HarperCollins, 1990).

Sprague, J. and D. Stuart, *The Speaker's Handbook,* 3rd ed. (New York: Harcourt Brace Jovanovich, 1992).

Value Debate Theory

Bahm, K., "Intrinsic Justificiation: Meaning and Method." *CEDA Yearbook,* 9 (1988): 23–29.

Berube, D. M., "Hasty Generalization Revisited, Part One: On Being Representative Examples." *CEDA Yearbook,* 10 (1989): 43–53.

Bile, J. T., "Propositional Justification: Another View." *CEDA Yearbook,* 9 (1988): 54–62.

Madsen, A. and R. C. Chandler, "When the Whole Becomes a Black Hole: Implications of the Holistic Perspective." *CEDA Yearbook,* 9 (1988): 30–37.

Matlon, R. J., "Debating Propositions of Value." *Journal of the American Forensic Association,* 14 (1978): 194–204.

Matlon, R. J., "Debating Propositions of Value: An Idea Revisited." *CEDA Yearbook,* 9 (1988): 1–14.

McGee, B., "Assessing Counter-Warrants: Understanding Induction in Debate Practice." *CEDA Yearbook,_9* (1988): 63–70.

Sellers, W., "On Reasoning About Values." *American Philosophical Quarterly,* 17 (1980): 81–101.

Verch, S. and B. Logue, "Increasing Value Clash: A Propositional and Structural Approach." *CEDA Yearbook,* (1982): 25–28.

Warnick, B., "Arguing Value Propositions." *Journal of the American Forensic Association,* 18 (1981): 109–119.

Wenzel, J. W., "Toward a Rationale for Value-Centered Argument." *Journal of the American Forensic Association,* 13 (1977): 150–158.

SUMMARY

This chapter introduces some of the considerable print resources available to forensics educators and a brief background of research in the field. There are many resources available to teachers, including printed books and articles, workshops, and handbooks. The chapter concludes with a bibliography of some of the materials available on subjects that teachers may be interested in. The next and final chapter of this text examines the subject of ethics in forensics.

ACTIVITIES

1. Create a bibliography of books and journals on forensics in your library. Is your collection reasonably up-to-date?
2. If students who have attended high school workshops or teachers who have sent students to workshops are available, talk with them. What are their reactions to their experiences? Would they recommend the workshop to other students?

NOTES

1. An excellent discussion of forensics research is found in *National Forensic Journal,* Spring, 1990.
2. Austin Freeley, *Argumentation and Debate.*
3. Ehninger and Brockriede, *Decision by Debate.*
4. Glen Mills, *Reason in Controversy.* (Boston: Allyn and Bacon, 1963).
5. Stephen Toulmin, *The Uses of Argument.* (Cambridge: University Press, 1958). Chaim Perelman and Lucie Olbrechts-Tyteca, *The New Rhetoric: A Treatise on Argumentation.* John Wilkinson Purcell Weaver, trans. (Notre Dame: University of Notre Dame Press, 1969).

6. Charles Willard, "Argument Fields and Theories of Logical Types." *Journal of the American Forensic Association*, 17 (1981): 129–145. "Special Issue: Review Symposium on Argument Fields." *Journal of the American Forensic Association*, 18 (1982): 191–257.

7. Published by the Alan Company.

8. See references to Alta Conferences and NFA Journal in bibliography section of this chapter.

9. Information on the *CEDA Yearbook* can be obtained through the Executive-Secretary of the Cross-Examination Debate Association.

10. Church and Wilbanks, Wood and Midgeley, Bartanen and Frank.

11. Dale Herbeck, "Debate Scholarship: A Needs Assessment." National Forensic Journal, 8 (1990): 1–16.

12. Austin Freeley, *Argumentation and Debate*.

13. Roy Wood and Lynn Goodnight, *Strategic Debate*, 4th ed. (Lincolnwood: National Textbook, 1989).

14. Mezzera and Giertz, *Student Congress and Lincoln-Douglas Debate*. Hunsaker, *Lincoln-Douglas Debate: Defining and Judging Value Debate*. Michael D. Bartanen and David A. Frank, *Lincoln-Douglas Debate: Preparation for a Lifetime of Arguing*. (Lincolnwood: National Textbook, 1993).

15. Thomas and Hart, *Advanced Debate*, 4th ed.

16. Fryar, Thomas, and Goodnight, *Basic Debate*, 2nd ed. Lynn Goodnight, *Getting Started in Debate*. These are two of the many textbooks available through the National Textbook Company.

17. Jo Sprague and Douglas Stuart, The Speaker's Handbook, 3rd ed. (New York: Harcourt Brace Jovanovich, 1992). C. T. Hanson, et al. *The Practice of Public Speaking: A Practical Guide for Beginning Speakers*, 2nd ed. (Dubuque: Kendall-Hunt, 1991).

18. Information about the *National Forensic Journal* can be ordered from the Secretary-Treasurer of the National Forensic Association. Currently (1992) Gerald A. Bluhm, Department of Speech, Marshall University, Huntington, WV, 25701 holds this position. Information about *The Forensic of Pi Kappa Delta* can be ordered from the Secretary-Treasurer of Pi Kappa Delta. Currently (1992) Harold Widvey, Department of Speech, South Dakota State University, Brookings, SD, 57007 holds this position.

19. Information about the *CEDA Yearbook* can be ordered from the Executive-Secretary of CEDA. Currently (1992) the Executive-Secretary is Michael Bartanen, Department of Communication and Theatre, Pacific Lutheran University, Tacoma, WA, 98447. Information about The Rostrum can be ordered from the National Forensic League office, Ripon, WI.

20. Information on SCA publications can be obtained from the national office in Annandale, VA.

21. ERIC, Educational Resources in Education, is a familiar educational resource.

22. Cat Horner Bennett, "NFL Conference on State of Debate: Are Debate Handbooks Proper Educational Materials for High School Debaters?" *The Forensic of Pi Kappa Delta*, 71 (1985): 13–18.

9
Ethical Issues in Forensics

CHAPTER OVERVIEW

This chapter discusses various ethical standards and ethical problems encountered in competitive forensics and traces the development of ethical standards in forensics. It then discusses ethical problems connected with forensics and divides those problems into various categories. The final section discusses attempts to address these problems through use of ethical codes.

Leaving a formal discussion of ethics until the final chapter in this textbook is a deliberate choice. It is not the last chapter because it is the least important, but it is a fitting place to bring together many issues discussed in this book. Without an appropriate and ethical perspective, most of the theories and strategies in this book will not produce the desired educational outcomes.

This chapter has three sections. The first is an overview of ethical principles in forensics, the second discusses some recurring ethical problems, and the final section consists of excerpts from several Codes of Ethics that are commonly used in competitive forensics.

AN OVERVIEW OF ETHICAL ISSUES IN FORENSICS

Discussion of ethical issues in communication is not a new subject. Scholars since at least Plato's time have studied and often disagreed about the ethical implications of speaking and arguing. Plato, in his work *Gorgias*,[1] was the first significant critic of the ethics of rhetoric.

Plato's philosophical system emphasized truth seeking through use of the dialectic process. People discovered truth by means of questions and answers designed to expose truth inductively. The dialectic process differed from the rhetorical process advocated by Aristotle and others. Rhetoric's emphasis was on persuasion instead of truth seeking. Aristotle emphasized the role of rhetoric in problem solving and decision-making. Rhetoric was conceived as a "practical" art.

The very practicality of rhetoric was also the source of Plato's main objections. Describing rhetoric as similar to "cookery," Plato saw a critical flaw in this method in the opportunity for rhetoricians to use it for immoral ends. Any method that could lead to outcomes other than the discovery of truth was indefensible.

This ethics dispute did not end in Greece. A concern for using rhetoric for ethical ends dominated Roman theory. Embracing a belief that the aim of rhetoric was to create a "good man speaking well" (remember that rhetoric was not taught to women), Roman rhetorical practices combined the studies of rhetoric and ethics and rejected the premise that the two studies were separable.

Saint Augustine preserved rhetoric from disappearing after the fall of the Roman Empire. He perceived the importance of rhetoric in disseminating Christian doctrine, and this led to the preservation of writings on rhetoric during the Middle Ages.[2]

Later, many prominent English rhetorical scholars also wrote extensively about the ethical ramifications of practice. Richard Whately, for example, was an Anglican bishop who introduced the concept of presumption to argumentation theory in the nineteenth century.[3] While Peter Ramus earlier divided rhetoric into two disciplines, the study of invention (philosophy) and the study of style and delivery (rhetoric), many writers continued to stress the importance of ethical principles to understanding and using rhetoric. Few of these writers were willing to consider rhetoric exclusively as a "neutral method" that did not depend on the speaker being ethical and honest.

Ethical debates accompanied the rising popularity of academic debate in the late nineteenth and early twentieth century. Some critics disdained debating both sides of the resolution, believing that such practice prevented students from developing their ability to argue in favor of the side representing their beliefs. Theodore Roosevelt was one of these critics.[4] This dispute lasted many years in the speech communication literature.

More recent ethical concerns about forensics have centered on competitive practices instead of the structure of the activity. As forensics became more complex as a competitive system the pressure to succeed engendered some ethically suspect practices. Those ethical concerns are discussed in the next section of this chapter.

RECURRING ETHICAL PROBLEMS IN CONTEMPORARY FORENSICS

Competition occasionally creates an incentive to cut corners. This unfortunate condition is true in every competitive circumstance. People break the rules in card games, baseball games, elections, and forensics contests. Games typically have rules to ensure fair play and ethical codes to encourage appropriate behavior in circumstances that the rules do not cover.

As you recall from the first part of this book, forensics has few rules guiding performance of the activity. Most of the rules pertain exclusively to the procedural conduct of the contests. These rules are supplemented by ethical codes created to encourage appropriate behavior. The difficulty with ethical codes is enforcing punishment for ethical violations. Most forensics organizations with ethical codes have applied sanctions reluctantly, fearing legal actions stemming from violations of due process rights. This fear of legal action makes ethical codes primarily advisory in nature, dependent on the willingness of people to adhere to the ethical standards.

There is no evidence that forensics is more susceptible to ethical problems than other competitive activities. Forensics has not endured the high profile criticism and scandal of television quiz shows, college athletic recruitment, or even religious fund-raising. In fact, many forensics educators and organizations spend substantial efforts in promoting high ethical standards. There is considerable discussion about whether particular practices and behaviors are ethically suspect. Rapid delivery in debate, for example, has long been addressed as an ethical problem. Although there is no consensus about its ethicality, the "debate" about "debate" shows the willingness of forensics educators to consider their practices from ethical perspectives.

We can divide ethical issues in forensics into three categories: interpersonal issues, scholarly issues, and competitive issues.

Interpersonal Issues

The first category is ethical problems stemming from forensics as a public communication activity. Common ethical problems of this type include

1. rapid delivery in debate
2. poor listening/audience behaviors

Rapid Delivery

No aspect of forensics is as controversial as rapid delivery in debate. The speaking rate during debates began escalating in the 1960s as information-processing models of debate became more popular. The strategy of using rapid delivery to increase the number of arguments presented is sometimes referred to as the "spread strategy." This strategy was fostered by judging models that rewarded teams for making arguments that the opposing team did not have time to respond to. The debate was considered a game where the quantity of arguments and claims became as important as the quality.

Several studies, and considerable anecdotal evidence, show that rapid delivery is a characteristic of many debates. Even debates where the speakers use more of a communication-oriented style are conducted at a delivery rate faster than normal conversation. Other debates, such as elimination rounds at national tournaments, are considerably faster than conversational delivery.[5]

Escalating delivery was one major reason for interest in high school Lincoln-Douglas debate and the CEDA organization at the college level. Unfortunately, the emphasis on slower delivery is no longer a universal characteristic of CEDA debates. Many of these debates are virtually indistinguishable in style and delivery rate from the NDT style debates for which they originally were an alternative.

In isolation, delivery rate is not unethical. Some evidence exists, for example, that audiences prefer faster to slower delivery in many communicative contexts.[6] Similarly, the motive for fast delivery often is to allow the speaker to present more arguments. This is an outgrowth of an increasingly information centered society where decision-makers rely heavily on information in their decision-making, even if that information is not necessarily relevant or helpful. Debate did not create a craving for information, but merely reflects a larger societal trend.

Rapid delivery is potentially both an ethical and strategic problem. It is an ethical problem if the motive for the rapid delivery is to embarrass or dehumanize the opponent. Debaters sometimes use rapid delivery as a verbal bludgeon, in an attempt to win solely on the fact that they present the most arguments instead the best ones. It would be similar to a professional basketball team using their superior athletic skills to run up the score on a high school team. Nothing in the rules would prohibit such behavior, but it would be highly ethically suspect.

On the other hand, some debate contexts and judges expect rapid delivery. Not adapting to a judge or a situation inevitably causes students to experience considerable frustration. The text has noted at several junctures the importance of audience adaptation. While we sometimes look at audience adaptation as a one-way street where fast debaters must adapt to slower judges, adaptation also goes in the other direction. No system can be considered truly open when some judges are not accorded the same consideration, through adaptation, simply because they prefer more rapid delivery. While judges should not be the only arbiter of standards in forensics, they are part of the equation for determining good versus bad practices. It is poor practice and even poorer philosophy to censor the views of any judge or listener who follow different standards.

Rapid delivery does have some strategic weaknesses also. A decrease in speaker comprehensibility often accompanies an increase in delivery rate. It is extremely difficult to articulate clearly at delivery rates that exceed normal conversation. Most speakers can, if they wish, speak rapidly. But without practice those speakers will likely be inarticulate. This makes it difficult for the judge to understand their arguments.

Another strategic weakness of rapid delivery is the inverse relationship between delivery rate and argument quality. The theory of rapid delivery is that it allows the debater to present a greater amount of good arguments that will ultimately persuade the judge to adopt the speaker's position. This is undoubtedly a fallacious position. All arguers, presumably, prioritize their arguments. They decide which arguments, positions, or issues will give them the greatest chance for success. If every argument or issue was equal in quality, rapid delivery would be obviously advantageous. In most circumstances, however, rapid delivery merely allows the arguer to present a great number of increasingly less valuable arguments.

To fill time debaters then rely on generic arguments applying to a variety of cases. This decreases clash in the debate and obscures the on-point arguments the debater is making. In a debate characterized by rapid delivery and generic arguments, debaters decrease their chances of success by presenting more arguments of less unique value. The more generic the argument, the more likely the opponent will have a satisfactory answer. The judge, having heard the same or a close variation of the generic argument, will less likely follow the unique arguments the debater advances.

Poor Listening/Interaction Skills

A second ethical problem is poor listening and interaction skills. A structural weakness of forensics as communication is the absence of audiences in most circumstances. Listening skills are only parenthetically taught in forensics. While good listening is very important in debate, because the speaker must respond to her opponent, it receives very little attention. In individual events, teachers place virtually complete emphasis on speaking as opposed to listening.

The focus in individual events competition is usually on performance variables. Time and attention are given to improving the presentation of the speech as a unilateral act. This is coupled with the growing trend toward students competing in many events simultaneously. Instead of having the chance to listen to other competitors, they are often hurrying to another round. Students are neither taught good listening skills nor given an opportunity to exercise them.

Poor listening is an ethical problem in two ways. First, it is obviously unethical for the listener to behave rudely while listening to a speaker.

Giving full attention to the speaker ought to be the duty of every listener. Instead, listeners will occasionally practice their own speech or do other distracting things. A second ethical problem is whether there ought to be a larger audience in a forensics round.

Double entry is the term describing competition where the individual events competitor can compete in multiple events happening simultaneously. A speaker, for instance, may present his persuasive speech, go immediately to his prose interpretation round, and then go compete in a third event! Double entry, rare in earlier times, is a common practice of many high school and college individual events tournaments.

Proponents justify double entry on economic and educational grounds. Economically, double-entry stretches scarce resources by giving competitors more speeches at a tournament. Since the costs of transportation, food, and lodging are relatively fixed, the more speeches a competitor can give, the greater justification there is for those fixed costs. With double entries, the program can get "more bang for the buck." Educationally, double entry presumably broadens competitors' experiences by encouraging them to prepare more speeches. These supposed advantages must be weighed in the contexts of the incurred costs.

First, double entry uses a competitive model that emphasizes the presentation of the speech as a unilateral act by a speaker instead of a shared act by speaker and audience. The goal of double entry is a quantitative increase in the number of speeches presented. The contest becomes, in a sense, an assembly line, where the judge processes individual speeches as complete acts.

An audience makes a fundamental difference to a speaking situation. While the judge is an audience there is a difference in speaking to one person as opposed to six or more. The speaker must adapt her physical delivery and her speaking content. Each member of the audience will respond differently to the speech and give the speaker different opportunities to improve her adaptation skills.

Lack of an audience also affects the total educational experience. While preparing multiple speeches may benefit the experienced speaker it is not clear whether less experienced competitors gain those same benefits. Observing other speakers is a helpful learning tool for speakers, so they can compare their performances and model their speaking on techniques used by more experienced speakers. They also can learn listening skills that will benefit them later in life.

There is no definitive answer as to whether the benefits of double entry outweigh its costs. While no doubt economically advantageous, it probably also is true that double entry excessively emphasizes the presentation of the speech at the expense of teaching audience adaptation skills.

Scholarly Issues

The second group of ethical problems arises from scholarship in forensics. Figure 9.1 lists these issues.

Forensics is a form of scholarship. The process of preparing a speech or a debate case is the same as writing a term paper. The speaker researches the topic, gathers information, then presents the supporting evidence. Good research skills are learned through study and trial. While building research skills is a major benefit of forensics training, it also presents ethical challenges.

Research ethics are a common problem in forensics. The nature of speech topics and debate resolutions makes sophisticated library research necessary. Students must read and understand complex books and articles on a subject area. They must frequently compare conflicting studies and evaluate subtle research methodologies. These skills are difficult for experienced researchers. They can be a particular challenge for high school or college students who do not have experience in research techniques.

This explains the high frequency of evidence problems in forensics as compared to other types of ethical problems. While there are no statistics about how frequently evidence problems occur, there is some indication that many speakers use evidence that is not completely accurate.[7]

There are several scholarship-related ethical problems. They include the falsification or deliberate distortion of evidence, misuse of evidence context, and unjust accusations of evidence misuse. Falsification of evidence is an absolute violation of all ethical codes. Deliberate distortion of evidence, through altering the wording, is also a serious ethical violation.

The difficulty of assessing distortion of evidence lies in finding the degree of the violation and the motivation of the distorter. Misinterpreting the context of evidence, of course, can range from minor to substantial misinterpretations. This misinterpretation also can result from lacking skill in evidence interpretation, making the offense unintentional.

Whatever the motive, however, speakers must take responsibility for their evidence usage. The judge or tournament has no way of assessing the

FIGURE 9.1 Ethical problems stemming from forensics as scholarship.

1. Misuse of evidence. Using a piece of evidence out of context of what the original author intended.
2. Falsification or distortion of evidence. Making up a piece of evidence or using the evidence inappropriately to support a position.
3. False accusation of evidence impropriety. Accusing another team or person of misusing evidence without proof.
4. Plagiarism. Using material written or researched by another person.

motivation. They must penalize the speaker when they find a piece of evidence out of context. Tournaments give the judge wide latitude in assessing a penalty for evidence misinterpretation. The judge can disregard the evidence, or give a lower rating or ranking to the speaker, or give a loss in the debate round. Normally, a student would not be disqualified from the tournament for misinterpreting evidence unless it was deliberate.

A similar ethical issue arises when an evidence challenge is made. Normally, this would happen only in a debate round. While it is within the rights of an opposing arguer to make an evidence challenge, we tend to expect that the accuser will present evidence to support his allegation. Making an evidence challenge without evidence may be considered as unethical as intentionally distorting evidence.

A speaker should never challenge evidence without proof to support the allegation. He should have a copy of the original book or article that contains the disputed evidence. In making a challenge, the accuser should carefully avoid assigning a motive for the behavior.

The final ethical problem connected with forensics as scholarship is the issue of plagiarism. Plagiarism addresses the question of who is responsible for creating arguments and speeches. Should a speaker read a speech or argument created by her teacher, another student, or from a debate handbook?

This is another area where there is disagreement about the ethical implications to forensics. There is an argument that teachers ought to be able to take an active role in the invention process. They do this to model good arguments and speeches. The invention process, particularly for the beginning student, can be very difficult. Furthermore, working with other students on speeches or arguments may represent a form of collaborative learning that is prized in many educational systems.

The standards on sharing arguments or speeches are clearer than similar standards for evidence usage we discussed earlier. There is no justification for teachers writing arguments or speeches for students. While the teacher ought to critique actively the students' work and suggest topics or arguments, the students must be primarily responsible for arguments or speeches they read. Reading the work of others, without attribution, is clearly plagiarism.

Less clear-cut are instances where several students or teams collaborate on arguments or speeches. If a student plays a role in creating the argument, she may use it safely. She is responsible, however, for any problems that may arise from evidence usage. This guideline also applies to individual events competition. It would be equally a form of plagiarism for a teacher to write a speech for the student or to cut an oral interpretation selection. Although the teacher may be more experienced as a speech writer, it remains the primary responsibility of the student to create arguments or speeches they read.

Some educators argue that since forensics is a competitive activity we should allow the teacher to create arguments or speeches. This is similar to the role of an athletic coach who creates plays that the competitors execute. This would be an appropriate model if the sole justification for forensics is as a competitive form. There is no theory, however, describing forensics purely in competitive terms. Every rationale for forensics places competition in a hierarchy with other values, such as education or social benefits. This hierarchy attempts to channel competition in productive ways and minimize the kinds of competitive excesses found in some athletic or other contexts.

Competitive Issues

The final category of ethical problems arises from forensics as a competitive form. Figure 9.2 lists some problems of this type.

We noted some pressures created by the competitive dynamics of forensics. Competition sometimes causes people to put aside their normal ethical instincts. Occasionally, teachers may perceive their job to depend on being competitively successful. Or individuals may simply feel that winning is everything and justifies any means.

Ethical problems stemming from competitive demands take three forms: unfair tournament processes, unfair judging practices, and unfair competitive practices. The tournament and the competitive round are the basic elements of forensics competition. The activity relies on participants believing that they have a fair chance to win and that the tournament, the judges, and the competitors are not attempting to manipulate the outcomes of the competition. Concerns about the competitive integrity of competition are not confined to forensics contests. Criticism of judging at Olympic contests in figure skating and boxing, for example, are common. Competitors and observers frequently assert that certain judges are biased

FIGURE 9.2 Ethical problems stemming from forensics as competition.

1. Unfair tournament processes. Problems relating to how tournament is operated, including scheduling, matching, or judge assignment.
2. Unfair judging practices. Problems relating to judge bias.
3. Unfair competitive processes. Problems related to events happening in a competitive round.
4. Recruiting of competitors. Problems related to the transferring of a student from one school to another.

against some competitors, or the tournament draw is weighted to favor others. These same concerns can be found in forensics contests.

It is easy to manipulate forensics tournaments in order to create a particular outcome. There are no set rules guiding the matching of competitive rounds. While most tournaments combine random matching and power-matching, there is always considerable room to influence the outcome through the "artistic choices" of the tournament managers. A tournament manager may choose to exchange the positions of two teams or two competitors, and often no one knows the difference.

A tournament also can affect outcomes through judge assignment. There are many judge assignment systems, including random, mutual preference, or strike influenced. A random system assigns judges randomly. The system only prevents a judge from listening to a contestant from her own school or hearing a student more than once in a tournament if avoidable. A mutual preference system, most often used in debates, allows teams to rate judges by placing them into preferential categories, such as *a*, *b*, or *c*. The tournament attempts to give each team in a debate an "a" judge or a "b" or "c," in descending order. The third system, the strike system, allows the team or contestant to list judges that they do not wish to judge them during the tournament. This system is usually used only in debate tournaments.

While theoretically the best system to preserve ethical standards obviously is the random system, it also presents the most opportunities for abuse. A random system gives the tournament the chance to favor some teams or contestants over others.

There are also ethical problems connected with judging practices. Just like the tournament, the judge is another one of the fundamental elements of the integrity of the activity. The judge is the sole arbiter of a forensics round. He need not defend his decision and can use any standards he wishes to evaluate a round. It is easy for a judge to influence the outcome of tournaments by making biased decisions. Unlike a legal system, a debate decision cannot be appealed. A biased judge can normally function with impunity as long as he does not admit to his bias.

Finally, the competitors themselves can behave in ethically suspect ways. A debate team, for example, can give analysis or evidence to another team to assist them in defeating a third team. In fact, "trading evidence and briefs" is a common competitive practice. As noted earlier, debaters or speakers are responsible for the material they present in a competitive round. However, there are no rules requiring them to disclose where they got the materials. The judge is expected to decide the round based on what is presented, not where it came from.

Trading evidence and briefs in this fashion undermines the ethical principles of the activity. Forensics only is justifiable when students are doing their own research and analysis. Relying on evidence or analysis created by others is not substantively different from any other form of plagiarism.

The final ethical problem in this category is recruitment of competitors. This is an ethical problem at the college level. Unlike college athletics, forensics does not have standard eligibility rules for students transferring from one school to another. CEDA is the only organization that regulates transfer students. They do not permit them to earn points for two semesters after they transfer from one four-year institution to another. This rule applies whatever the reasons are for the transfer.

Blatantly recruiting a student to transfer schools is recognized as patently unethical.[8] It is, unfortunately, more difficult to ascertain when more subtle recruiting occurs. This recruiting takes the form of students recruiting other students, or students being attracted to another school for other reasons. Some argue that students have a right to transfer schools regardless of the reason.[9] This is undoubtedly true and is essential to freedom of association.

On the other hand, forensics competition is not a "right" but a "privilege" associated with meeting the rules of colleges, high schools, and relevant organizations. Rules regulating transfer eligibility of high school students have been upheld in the courts. Relevant college rules do not inhibit the right of students to compete. The rules attempt to ensure a "level playing field" by minimizing the competitive advantage a program receives by having a student transfer into its program.

Unlike other activities, forensics has few rules and relies on norms generated from ethical codes and other sources. The next section briefly details some ethical standards appropriate for use in forensics activities.

ETHICAL STANDARDS IN FORENSICS

This section presents some ethical standards for forensics and some excerpts from ethical codes. As noted in the previous section, there is no total consensus regarding the nature of ethical standards or problems in forensics. Competitive strategies can sometimes be labeled as ethical violations. Given the lack of absolute standards for evaluating forensics practices, use of an ethical framework is essential.

There are several ethical frameworks we may apply to evaluating forensics practices. They include an interpersonal-based ethic, a message-based ethic, and an absolutist ethic. Figure 9.3 lists the major focus of each of these frameworks.

These categories are not mutually exclusive. They emphasize different ethical aspects. Forensics relies primarily on interpersonal- or message-

FIGURE 9.3 Ethical frameworks and their major focus.

FRAMEWORK	FOCUS
Interpersonal	Evaluates ethical questions on the basis of their effects on other people.
Message	Evaluates the ethics of messages through evaluating their fairness or appropriateness.
Absolutist	Evaluates ethical questions by applying universal standards.

based ethical standards. The previous section gives some insight to the difficulty of applying absolutist standards. Violations are rarely easy to categorize and there are considerable disagreements about the ethics of various practices. Situational standards, such as interpersonal- and message-based ethical guidelines, are more appropriate for evaluating the kinds of ethical problems associated with the activity.

Interpersonal Based

An *interpersonal-based ethic* considers ethics from the perspective of how a practice affects the rights and humanity of other individuals. Practices are ethically suspect when they intend to dehumanize individuals. Wayne Brockriede outlined this perspective in several articles. In "Arguers as Lovers" (1972), Brockriede used the love-making metaphor to distinguish between various ethical behaviors.[10] He identified argumentative stances including the argumentative "rapist," "seducer," and "lover." The rapist and seducer considered other people as objects to be manipulated through coercion or trickery. They consider winning to be important at any cost and the rights of the individual unimportant.

The argumentative lover views argument as a transaction between equals. The lover is concerned enough about the argument to try hard but is not consumed with winning to the extent of sacrificing the other person. This perspective demands that the arguer commit to the possibility of being proved wrong. This perspective is a useful one for evaluating forensics ethics. It distinguishes between the kinds of ethical problems that are gratuitous, as opposed to ones that are malicious or premeditated.[11] Many ethical problems arise from ignorance or short-sighted scholarship and not from malice or premeditation.

Other ethical problems connected with debate as scholarship are gratuitous in nature. When there is indication that the violation is malicious or premeditated, revealing that the arguer is treating others as "objects," a more substantial ethical violation occurs. Teachers then have the responsibility to impose greater sanctions against acts that fall into that category.

Message Based

A second ethical standard is a *message-based* standard. This is a traditional ethical standard grounded in traditional rhetorical principles. Both the Greeks and Romans were highly concerned with creating ethical speakers and ethical arguments. Building on those traditions, Karl Wallace reintroduced a message-based ethical standard known as "good reasons."[12] This standard emphasizes the ethical duty of the speaker to use the most powerful and ethical reasons available in a persuasive context. This standard would place greater emphasis on creating ethical messages, as opposed to making ethical ones about interactions with others. This standard would penalize speakers using out-of-context evidence or misapplied arguments. The standard relies on the ability of the judge to weigh carefully evidence and message content.

Both standards create definite ethical obligations for forensics participants. These obligations include the following.

1. *Forensics competitors ought to behave humanely toward other competitors.* Any practice that intends to dehumanize other individuals is ethically suspect. This includes actions such as biased language, disrespectful speaking and listening behaviors, or unfair competitive practices.

2. *Forensics competitors ought to be the primary creators and discoverers of evidence and analysis.* Forensics competitors are responsible for evidence and analysis they use in speeches and debates. Their education is best served when they gather their own evidence and write their own claims. The role of the teacher ought to be to critique student efforts rather than to take a primary role in creating evidence, arguments, or speeches.

3. *Forensics contests should meet the highest standards of fair play.* Tournaments and particular rounds should be run fairly and should give no competitor an artificial advantage. Tournaments must scrupulously avoid the perception of favoritism. Judges should take their judging responsibilities seriously and behave fairly. Judges ought to judge various events and develop high standards that the competitors know in advance.

4. *Education, rather than competition, ought to be the primary focus of forensics.* Ethical problems inevitably result when competition is overemphasized. The highest ethical standards are achieved when competition is a means rather than an end. Overemphasizing competition causes students and programs to place expediency over fairness and undermines the educational rationale for the activity.

SUMMARY

This chapter examines ethics and ethical problems in forensics. It identifies three types of ethical problems: interpersonal, scholarly, and competitive. It then discusses some standards that can be used to evaluate ethical problems in forensics, which include ethical standards based on interpersonal needs and universal "good reasons." The appendix to this chapter gives an example of ethical codes from the Code of Ethics of the American Forensic Association. The code illustrates the ways that these organizations attempt to codify ethical practices. Other forensics organizations also have ethical codes that you would do well to consult.

ACTIVITIES

1. Discuss the three ethical standards introduced in this chapter. Which one fits more comfortably with your personal ethical framework? Which one would work best for assessing ethical standards in forensics?

2. Discuss how you would help students recognize problems in scholarship. How can teachers help students become more accurate and skillful at finding and applying evidence in debate cases and individual events speeches?

3. How can a teacher justify high ethical standards when other students and programs may be successful for using ethically suspect practices?

NOTES

1. Plato, *Georgias*. In W.K.C. Guthrie, *A History of Greek Philosophy*. (Cambridge: Cambridge University Press, 1969–1978).
2. Kennedy, *Classical Rhetoric and Its Christian and Secular Tradition from Ancient to Modern Times*.
3. Richard Whately, *The Elements of Rhetoric*. Douglas Ehninger, ed. (Carbondale: Southern Illinois University Press, 1963).
4. This controversy is discussed by E. R. Nichols, "A Historical Sketch of Inter-Collegiate Debating: I, II." *Quarterly Journal of Speech*, 22 (1936): 213–220, 591–602.
5. Kent R. Colbert, "Speaking Rated of N.D.T. finalists from 1968–1980." Journal of the American Forensic Association, 18 (1981): 73–76.

6. Studies of delivery seem to support the idea that audiences lend greater credibility to a speaker whose rate exceeds normal conversational delivery speed than a speaker whose rate falls below normal delivery speed.

7. Robert Frank, "The Abuse of Evidence in Persuasive Speaking." *National Forensic Journal*, 1 (1983): 97–109. David Thomas and Jack Hart, "Ethics in Speech Events: A Replication and Extension." *National Forensic Journal*, 1 (1983): 74–96. B. K. Duffy, "The Ethics of Argumentation in Intercollegiate Debate: A Conservative Appraisal." *National Forensic Journal*, 1 (1983): 65–71.

8. Parson, *American Forensics in Perspective*.

9. Michael Bartanen, "The Case for Regulation of Forensic Transfers." *The Forensic of Pi Kappa Delta*, 73 (1988): 1–6. Brian McGee and Greggory Simerly, "In Defense of Unregulated Forensics Transfers: A Response to Bartanen." *The Forensic of Pi Kappa Delta*, 76 (1991): 6–11.

10. Wayne Brockriede, "Arguers as Lovers." *Philosophy and Rhetoric*, 5 (1972): 1–11.

11. Kristine M. Davis, "Ethics of Individual Events Coaching: Getting a Leg Up on the Competition." Presented to Northwest Communication Association, Coeur d'Alene, ID, 1983.

12. Karl Wallace, "The Substance of Rhetoric: Good Reasons." *Quarterly Journal of Speech*, 49 (1963): 239–249.

Code of Ethics of the American Forensic Association

American Forensic Association
Professional Relations Committee
Code of Forensics Program and
Forensics Tournament Standards
for Colleges and Universities
(Adopted 1982)

PREFACE

The American Forensic Association, as a professional organization for forensics educators, believes that forensics programs and tournaments ought to provide environments where students can become intelligent, effective, and responsible advocates and communicators.

We believe in equality and fair play in all forensics competition, and we therefore promulgate the following Code of Forensics Program and Forensics Tournament Standards for Colleges and Universities in the hopes that the guidelines outlined here will serve to govern and regulate effectively the conduct of forensics competition in the United States.

Article I: Competitor Standards

1. A tournament contestant is to be an officially enrolled undergraduate student in good standing at the college or university he/she is representing in forensics competition.

A. A contestant is considered "officially enrolled" when he/she is duly registered in accordance with institutional regulations as an undergraduate student at the college or university he/she is representing in competition.

B. A contestant is considered an "undergraduate" if he/she is registered as a bachelor or associate degree seeking student at the institution he/she is to represent in competition and is not in possession of a Bachelor's degree.

C. "Good standing" shall be determined by rules and policies set by the institution the forensics competitor is representing in competition.

2. A tournament contestant is eligible for competition in a maximum of eight time blocks:

A. A time bloc is:

(1) July—December

(2) January—June

B. A student shall have used his/her eligibility in a given time block if he/she participates in three or more forensics tournaments:

(1) A student shall be considered to have participated in a tournament if he/she competes in at least half of the scheduled preliminary rounds of the tournament.

(2) A tournament is defined as a forensics contest involving at least four schools in which at least four rounds of debate or two rounds of individual events are held, decisions are rendered by judges, and awards given. This definition does not include summer workshop tournaments.

(3) A student's participation in individual events shall not count against his/her eligibility to compete in debate, and vice-versa.

3. Students are free to transfer from one college to another so long as the transfer is not the result of an unscrupulous effort by one school to cause the student to transfer to it in order to receive financial compensation and/or other rewards for forensics competition.

A. "Unscrupulous" is used here to refer to cases where the college that the student transfers to *initiates* contact with the student and makes an offer of financial compensation and/or other rewards for forensic competition if the student transfers.

B. The PRC will determine if a student's transfer is the result of unscrupulous recruiting efforts based on the facts of the individual case. It is the burden of the school alleging unscrupulous recruiting to provide proof to the PRC that the school that the student transfers to initiated the contact with the student and the decision to transfer was motivated by the promise of financial compensation and/or other rewards for forensic competition.

4. Under unusual circumstances, involving valid educational or professional justifications, students who have received bachelor degrees may participate if:

A. The student has never competed in forensics as an undergraduate.

B. The coach who desires to let the student compete informs chair of the PRC of this decision and the reasons for it, and a majority of the PRC agrees that the student has valid educational or professional reasons for participating.

C. Such students may participate for a maximum of two time blocks.

D. The above eligibility rules shall not restrict additional eligibility requirements established by either the NDT or NIET Committees or by individual tournament directors.

Article II: Competitor Practices

1. Forensics competitors shall not use fabricated or distorted evidence.
    A. Evidence is defined as factual material (statistics and examples) and/or opinion testimony offered as proof of a debater's or a speaker's contention, claim, position, argument, point, or case.
    B. Fabrication of evidence refers to falsely representing a cited fact or statement of opinion as evidence when the material in question is not authentic. Fabricated evidence is so defined without reference to whether or not the debater or speaker using it was the person responsible for fabricating it.
    C. Distorted evidence refers to misrepresenting the actual or implied content of factual or opinion evidence. Distorted evidence is so defined without reference to whether or not the debater or speaker using it was the person responsible for distorting it. Distortions shall be judged by comparing the challenged evidence against the material as it appears in the original source. Distortions include, but are not limited to:
        (1) quoting out of context.
        (2) misinterpreting the evidence so as to alter its meaning.
        (3) omitting salient information from quotations or paraphrases. MLA Standards will be considered advisory with respect to this standard.
        (4) adding words to a quotation that were not present in the original source of the evidence without identifying such an addition.
        (5) failure to provide complete documentation of the evidence (name[s] of author[s], source of publication, full date, page numbers and author[s] credentials where available in the original when challenged.
    Debaters and speakers are expected to be in possession of the forms of documentation listed here at the time they used any evidence that was challenged.
2. In individual events that involved original student speech compositions (oratory/persuasion, informative/expository, after-dinner/speech to entertain/epideictic, rhetorical criticism/communication analysis, impromptu,

extemporaneous, or other similar speaking contests), the speaker shall not commit plagiarism.

   A. Plagiarism is defined as claiming another's written or spoken words as one's own, or claiming as one's own a significant portion of the creative work of another.

   B. A speech in individual events competition is considered plagiarized when the student presenting it was not the principal person responsible for researching, drafting, organizing, composing, refining, and generally constructing the speech in question.

3. Forensics competitors are expected to do their own research.

   A. Persons other than the forensic competitor (undergraduate students, graduate student, or instructor/coaches) are not to be charged with the responsibility for doing a forensics competitor's research.

   B. This provision shall not be construed to prevent coaches or assistants from engaging in limited research designed to:

       (1) teach research techniques,

       (2) provide limited examples of high quality research,

       (3) identify areas of research that students should pursue, and

       (4) provide the coach with the working knowledge necessary to function as effective critic with respect to the debate or speech topics being investigated by his/her students.

4. All forensics participants are expected to compete honestly and fairly. Students are not to intentionally lose debates or perform badly in individual events rounds for the purpose of allowing other competitors to benefit as a result. Directors of forensics, judges, and coaches are not to encourage dishonesty in competition by asking students to purposely lose or do poorly in rounds of forensics competition.

Article III: Tournament Practices

1. Tournament directors must ensure that all participants compete on a more or less equal basis.

   A. A debate team should not meet the same team twice during preliminary rounds of a tournament unless:

       (1) There are so few teams entered that it would be impossible for the tournament to proceed, in which case the two teams would switch sides the second time they meet, or

       (2) The schools entering the tournament have agreed to suspend the provision that teams not debate each other twice in preliminary rounds.

   B. So far as possible, debate teams should debate an equal number of preliminary rounds on each side of the debate proposition.

   C. Speakers in individual events shall not by repeatedly matched against the same opponents in a given event, unless:

       (1) the tournament cannot proceed otherwise, or

(2) the schools attending the tournament agree to suspend the provision that speakers should not repeatedly meet the same opponents in a given round of individual events.

D. So far as possible, speakers in individual events contests should rotate speaking positions.

E. Judges for forensics contests shall be assigned in accordance with these stipulations:

(1) A judge shall not be assigned to judge his/her own team.

(2) A judge shall not judge the same debate team or student speaker in one particular individual event twice during a tournament's preliminary rounds unless there is no way to avoid this conflict.In such cases:

   (a) the judge will hear the debate team on the opposite side, unless it is impossible to do this or the schools competing agree to suspend this provision, and

   (b) the judge will hear the student speaker compete against as many different opponents than those involved in the judge's first hearing of the speech, unless it is impossible to do this or the schools competing agree to suspend this provision.

(3) A judge shall not judge debaters or speakers where there is a conflict of interest possible, such as:

   (a) The judge has previously coached in college a debater or speaker he/she is to hear.

   (b) The judge was, within the last two years, the coach of the school whose team or speaker he/she is to hear.

   (c) The judge was, within the last two years, an undergraduate student forensics competitor at the school whose team or speaker he/she is to hear.

(4) Prior to the start of the tournament, all judges shall have an opportunity to declare themselves ineligible to hear specific debate teams, speakers, or events.

(5) The practice of allowing debate teams or individual events speakers to prevent a specific judge from hearing a particular team or speaker is permitted only when:

   (a) all teams or speakers are given an equal chance to declare judge strikes prior to the start of the tournament,

   (b) all teams and speakers are granted the same number of strikes—the number to be determined by the tournament director(s), and

   (c) the procedures for removing strikes (if any) are stated openly to all competitors.

2. Tournaments should be completely and fairly advertised.

A. The levels of competition expected should be specified.

B. If the tournament has more than one division of competition, eligibility requirements for the divisions shall be clearly defined in the tournament invitation.

C. The basis for advancing competitors to the elimination rounds, and/or for awarding trophies or prizes, shall be specified either in the tournament invitation or in written or oral statements presented to all tournament participants prior to the start of the first round of the tournament.

D. The rules governing all competitive events (event description, procedures, time limits, etc. shall be clearly specified in the tournament invitation.

3. All tournament rounds are open on a space available basis to any and all interested observers, who may take notes. Participants, coaches of the teams involved, judges, or authorized researchers (with the tournament director's approval) may tape record any tournament round of competition.

4. Tournament judges are obliged to provide detailed and constructive criticism of any and all rounds of competition they evaluate. Judges are expected to provide written comments on the ballots provided by the tournament. These written comments should be made available to all the competitors a judge has heard by the conclusion of the tournament. All provisions of this article shall apply to high school and college competitors.

5. Tournament directors should ensure that:
A. Results are made available to all contestants as soon after competition ends as is humanly possible.

B. Their tournament is not run to benefit financially the host school. And anticipated profit in excess of 10 percent of total entry fees is considered excessive.

C. Their tournament runs smoothly and efficiently, with breaks in between rounds for power-matching minimized whenever possible.

D. All results are kept secret *if that is specified by the tournament rules.*

Article IV: Adjudication Procedures

1. Anyone wishing to initiate a formal complaint may do so by sending SIX copies of the charges, in writing, to the Chair of the PRC.
The complaint must:
A. Indicate the specific section(s) of the Code allegedly violated.

B. Name the person(s) charged with the alleged violation(s).

C. Indicate the factual circumstances and events associated with the alleged violation(s).

D. Include all necessary supporting documents that would constitute at least a *prima facie* case that there is reason to believe that a violation of the Code may have occurred.

E. Include the addresses and phone numbers of the person making the complaint.

2. The PRC, upon receipt of SIX copies of the charges, will inform, in writing, the person charged with an alleged code violation. The person(s) charged will have 30 days to respond to the charges. The person charged will be informed of the nature and extent of the charges against him/her. The person charged may supply any relevant information in his/her defense in regard to the charges. SIX copies of any material supplied should be sent to the Chair of the PRC.

3. Once all materials are gathered, the PRC members will independently review the case and determine if there is reason to believe that a code violation has occurred.

    A. If the PRC agrees, by majority vote, that there is insufficient proof of a violation, the charges will be declared dropped and all parties to the dispute informed.

    B. If the PRC agrees, by majority vote, that there is sufficient evidence to support the charges made, the Chair of the PRC will inform all parties of this fact and will schedule a formal hearing as soon as possible involving the members of the PRC, the accused, and the person bringing the complaint. The location of this hearing will be determined by the Chair of the PRC, with the location being as convenient as possible to all parties. The hearing shall occur as soon as it can be feasibly scheduled. The accused will have the right to make an oral defense at the hearing, and can be represented by legal counel if desired. The complainant will have the same rights. At the conclusion of the hearing, the PRC will vote on the charges. At least a 4–1 vote is required to convict the accused of a Code violation. Following the verdict of guilty, the PRC will determine the penalties to be imposed in accordance with Article V of the Code. A majority vote will be required to impose penalties.

4. The accused may appeal both the verdict and the penalties determined by the PRC.

    A. The appeal will be made to the President of the AFA, who will appoint a special three-person appeal board composed of impartial members of the AFA.

    B. The appeal board will review all documents gathered by the PRC, and will also listen to tape-recordings of the formal hearings.

    C. The appeal board may gather any additional information it deems necessary to judge the case from any of the parties (the accused), the complainant, or the PRC.

    D. The accused and the complainant have the right to present an oral argument to the appeal board. If so desired, the appeal board will set up a convenient method for allowing either the accused or the complainant to address it. The accused and the complainant have the right to counsel in these instances.

E. A majority vote of the appeal board is necessary to overturn the PRC's actions.

Article V: Penalties

1. Directors of forensics, assistants or coaches found guilty of entering ineligible students in forensics competition will:
   A. Have their names published in *AFA Newsletter* with a note of censure.
   B. Have the notice of censure conveyed in writing by the AFA President to appropriate officials at the offending institution.

2. A student declared ineligible will be barred from national competitions or awards sponsored in whole or in part by the AFA. Notice of this action will be published in the *AFA Newsletter*, with a letter sent by the AFA President to appropriate officials at the offending student's school informing them of the student's ineligibility for competition in forensics.

3. In instances of evidence distortion and/or fabrication, the judge(s) shall automatically award the decision in the debate to the opposing team and give the offending speaker zero speaker points, noting the violation of the rules of evidence on the ballot as the reason for the judges' decision and points. In individual events, the judge(s) will treat evidence distortion and/or fabrication by giving the offending speaker zero points and by dropping that speaker from the speaker rankings to be assigned at the end of the round. The judge(s) will note the violation of the rules of evidence on the ballot as the reason for the points and no-rank given.

4. Speakers found guilty of plagiarism will be disqualified from the round in which the plagiarism occurred, with zero speaker points and no rank assigned and plagiarism noted on the ballot as the reason for the judge's action.

5. A judge who makes a decision on the basis of evidence distortion, evidence fabrication, or plagiarism will immediately report his/her action to the tournament director. The tournament director will, as soon as possible, investigate the incident and determine if the offending speaker should be declared ineligible for further competition, elimination rounds, or awards at the tournament. Directors should base such decisions on the severity of the case involved.

6. Tournament directors must report, to the Chair of the PRC, any and all instances of judge decisions granted for reasons of evidence distortion, evidence fabrication, or plagiarism. If the Chair receives in any given academic year, two such complaints involving the same student, the student will be declared ineligible for national competitions or awards sponsored in whole or in part by the AFA for a period of 12 calendar months from the date of the second offense. The student will be informed when notification of the second offense is received. The student has the right to appeal that the penalty should not be imposed, under the appeal procedure outline in Article IV, Section 4 of this code. Notice of the student's ineligibility for national competitions sponsored by the AFA will appear

in the *AFA Newsletter,* with a letter by the AFA President sent to appropriate officials at the offending student's school.

7. Forensics squads found guilty of using non-competitors for primarily research purposes will have a note of censure published in the *AFA Newsletter,* with written notice of the censure communicated by the AFA President to appropriate officials at the offending school. The squad will be barred from national competitions sponsored in whole or in part by the AFA for a period of 12 calendar months from the date when the PRC ruled the school to be in violation of this part of the Code.

8. Tournament directors found guilty of violating any section of Article III of this Code will be subject to any or all of the sanctions listed below, as deemed justified by the PRC:

   A. Censure of the offending tournament.

      (1) The PRC finding that the tournament had violated the Code will be published in the *AFA Newsletter.*

      (2) Appropriate officials at the offending school will be notified in writing by the AFA President of the decision to censure the tournament.

      (3) In cases where the PRC determines the Code violation to be severe, the tournament will not be allowed to publish its dates in the next AFA tournament calendar following the PRC's decision that the tournament was in violation of the Code.

   B. Tournament Probation.

      (1) When a tournament is found guilty of a Code violation on a second separate occasion, the tournament may be put on probation; viz. The results of the *next* occurrence of the tournament, following the PRC's decision to place it on probation, cannot be used for the purpose of qualifying forensic participants for national tournaments sponsored in whole or in part by the AFA.

      (2) If a tournament is placed on probation, this decision will be printed in the *AFA Newsletter* Tournament Calendar edition covering the tournament season in which the probation will be served, with notification that this tournament's results cannot be used for the purpose of qualifying forensic students for national competitions sponsored in whole or in part by the AFA.

      (3) Probation will be for one year. When the probation ends that fact will be reported in the *AFA Newsletter* Tournament Calendar issue.

9. Tournament directors should forward names of all judges who fail to turn in written ballots for all the preliminary rounds they judge at a tournament to the Chair of the PRC. Any school that leaves a tournament without all of the preliminary round ballots it should have, and assuming there is no valid explanation for missing ballots, may notify the Chair of the PRC of the judge(s) who failed to provide ballots. If a judge is guilty of failing to

provide written preliminary round ballots for all rounds judged by the end of the tournament on two occasions, the judge shall be:

A. Subject to censure by notification in the *AFA Newsletter*, and be

B. Declared ineligible to be hired as a judge at any national competition sponsored in whole or in part by the AFA, and be

C. Informed when notification of the second failure to turn in ballots is received. The judge may appeal that the penalty should not be imposed, under the appeal procedures outlined in Article IV, Section 4 of the Code.

10. Forensics directors, coaches, assistants, or judges found guilty of asking students to throw rounds of forensics competition will be subject to the penalties listed under Section 1 of this Article.

11. A student transferring from one school to another as a consequence of unscrupulous recruiting will be ineligible to participate in the next national tournament sponsored in whole or in part by the AFA occurring after the PRC's decision that the transfer resulted from unscrupulous contact initiated by the school to which the student transferred.

Works Cited

Aristotle, *The Rhetoric.* In R. Robert, trans., *The Works of Aristotle.* (Oxford: Clarendon Press, 1924).

Bacon, Wallace A., *The Art of Interpretation,* 2nd ed. (New York: Holt, Rinehart and Winston, 1972).

Bartanen, Kristine M., "Use of Criteria Referenced Ballots for Individual Events." *National Forensic Journal,* 8 (1991): 133–144.

Bartanen, Michael, "The Case for Regulation of Forensic Transfers." *The Forensic of Pi Kappa Delta,* 73 (1988): 1–6.

Bartanen, Michael and David A. Frank, *Debating Values.* (Scottsdale: Gorsuch Scarisbrick, 1990).

Bartanen, Michael and David A. Frank, "The Issue-Agenda Model." *The Forensic,* 69 (1983): 1–9.

Bartanen, Michael and David A. Frank, *Lincoln-Douglas Debate: Preparation for a Lifetime of Value Argumentation.* (Lincolnwood: National Textbook, 1993).

Bennett, Cat Horner, "NFL Conference on State of Debate: Are Debate Handbooks Proper Educational Materials for High School Debators?" *The Forensic of Pi Kappa Delta,* 71 (1985): 13–18.

Benson, James A., "Extemporaneous Speaking: Organization Which Inheres." *Journal of the American Forensic Association,* 14 (1978): 150–155.

Berger, Charles R., "Task Performance and Attributional Communication as Determinants of Interpersonal Attraction." *Speech Monographs,* 40 (1973): 280–286.

Bile, Jeffrey, "When the Whole Is Greater than the Sum of the Parts: The Implications of Holistic Resolutional Focus." *CEDA Yearbook,* (1987): pp. 8–15.

Brockriede, Wayne, "Arguers as Lovers." *Philosophy and Rhetoric,* 5 (1972): 1–11.

Brown, W. and P. Swisher, *Directing Successful Speech Tournaments.* (Grandview: Dale Publishing, 1980).

Carmack, Paul A., "The Development of State High School Speech Leagues." *The Speech Teacher,* III (1954): 264–268.

Clarke, M. L., *Higher Education in the Ancient World.* (London: Routledge and Kegan, 1971).

Colbert, Kent and Thompson Biggers, "Why Should We Support Debate?" *Journal of the American Forensic Association,* 21 (1985): 237–240.

Colbert, Kent R., "The Effects of CEDA and NDT Debate Training on Critical Thinking Ability." *Journal of the American Forensic Association,* 23 (1987): 194–201.

Colbert, Kent R., "Speaking Rates of NDT Finalists from 1968 to 1980." *Journal of the American Forensic Association,* 18 (1981): 73–76.

Davis, Kristine M., "In Defense of the Value Oration." *The Forensic of Pi Kappa Delta,* 68 (1982): 602.

Davis, Kristine M., "Ethics of Individual Events Coaching: Get a Leg up on the Competition," presented to the Northwest Communication Association, Couer d'Alene, Idaho, 1983.

Dean, Kevin W. and Kenda Creasy Dean, "Forensic Recruiting Within the University." *National Forensic Journal,* 3 (1985): 37–54.

Duffy, B. K., "The Ethics of Argumentation in Intercollegiate Debate: A Conservative Appraisal." *National Forensic Journal,* 1 (1983): 65–71.

Ehninger, Douglas and Wayne Brockriede, *Decision by Debate,* (New York: Dodd, Mead, 1963).

Endres, Thomas G., "Maintaining Integrity in Forensics Interpretation: Arguments Against Original Literature." *National Forensic Journal,* 6 (1988): 89–102.

Faules, Donald F., Richard D. Rieke, and Jack Rhodes, *Directing Forensics: Contest and Debate Speaking,* 2nd ed. (Denver: Morton Publishing, 1976).

Foss, Sonja K., *Rhetorical Criticism: Exploration and Practice.* (Prospect Heights: Waveland, 1989).

Frank, Robert, "The Abuse of Evidence in Persuasive Speaking." *National Forensic Journal,* 1 (1983): 97–109.

Freeley, Austin J., *Argumentation and Debate,* 6th ed. (Belmont: Wadsworth, 1986).

Fryar, Maridell, David Thomas, and Lynn Goodnight, *Basic Debate,* 2nd ed. (Lincolnwood: National Textbook, 1989).

Geisler, Deborah, "Modern Interpretation Theory and Competitive Forensics: Understanding Hermeneutic Text." *National Forensic Journal,* 3 (1985): 71–79.

Goodnight, G. T. and D. Zarefsky, *Forensics Tournaments: Planning and Administration.* (Lincolnwood: National Textbook, 1980).

Goodnight, Lynn, *Getting Started in Debate.* (Lincolnwood: National Textbook).

Green, Keith D., "Original Material in Forensics Oral Interpretation: A Violation of Integrity." *National Forensic Journal,* 6 (1988): 63–72.

Guthrie, W. K. C., *A History of Greek Philosophy.* (Cambridge: University Press, 1969–1978).

Hanson, C. T., "What Are the Options: The Philosophy of Using Ballots." *The Forensic of Pi Kappa Delta,* 74 (1988): 1–6.

Hanson, C. T. et al. *The Practice of Public Speaking: A Practical Guide for Beginning Speakers,* 2nd ed. (Dubuque: Kendall-Hunt, 1991).

Hart, Roderick, and Don Burks, "Rhetorical Sensitivity and Social Interaction." *Communication Monographs,* 39 (1972): 75–91.

Herbeck, Dale, "Debate Scholarship: A Needs Assessment." *National Forensic Journal,* 8 (1990): 1–16.

Hill, Bill, "Intercollegiate Debate: Why Do Students Bother?" *Southern Speech Communication Journal,* 48 (1982: 77–88.

Howe, Jack H. "CEDA's Objectives: Lest We Forget." *CEDA Yearbook 1981: The Philosophy and Practice of CEDA.*

Hunsaker, Richard A., *Lincoln-Douglas Debate: Defining and Judging Value Debate.* (Kansas City: National Federation of State High School Assns., 1988).

Huseman, R. C. and D. M. Goodman, "Editor's Corner: BYD Congressional Questionnaire." *Journal of the American Forensic Association,* 12 (1976): 226.

Kelly, Beverly, "An Alternative to NDT Debate." *CEDA Yearbook 1981: The Philosophy and Practice of CEDA,* pp. 8–14.

Kennedy, George A., *Classical Rhetoric and Its Christian and Secular Tradition from Ancient to Modern Times.* (Chapel Hill: University of North Carolina Press, 1980).

Larson, Charles U., *Persuasion: Reception and Responsibility,* 6th ed. (Belmont: Wadsworth, 1992).

Lee, Charlotte, *Oral Interpretation,* 6th ed. (Boston: Houghton Mifflin, 1986).

Lewis, Todd V., "The Performance of Literature at Forensics Tournaments: A Case for the Use of Original Material." *National Forensic Journal,* 6 (1988): 63–72.

Littlefield, Robert S., "An Assessment of University Administrators: Do They Value Competitive Debate and Individual Events Programs?" *National Forensic Journal,* 9 (1991): 87–96.

Lord, Albert A., *The Singer of Tales.* (New York: Atheneum, 1960).

McBath, James H., ed. *Forensics as Communication: The Argumentative Perspective.* (Skokie: National Textbook, 1975): p. 11.

McBath, James H. "Speech and the Legal Profession." *Speech Teacher,* 10 (1961): 44–47.

McGee, Brian and Gregory Simerly, "In Defense of Unregulated Forensics Transfers: A Response to Bartanen." *The Forensic of Pi Kappa Delta,* 76 (1991): 6–11.

McGough, M. "Pull It Across Your Flow." *The New Republic,* 199 (1988): 17–19.

McGregor, Douglas, *The Human Side of Enterprise.* (New York: McGraw-Hill, 1960).

Mezzera, David and John Giertz, *Student Congress and Lincoln-Douglas Debate,* 2nd ed. (Lincolnwood: National Textbook, 1989).

Mills, Glen, *Reason in Controversy.* (Boston: Allyn and Bacon, 1963).

Murphy, James J., *A Synoptic History of Classical Rhetoric.* (New York: Random House, 1972).

Nadler, Marjorie Keeshan, "The Gender Factor in Selecting Extra-Curricular Activities." *National Forensic Journal,* 3 (1985): 29–36.

Nichols, E. R., "A Historical Sketch of Intercollegiate Debating: I, II." *Quarterly Journal of Speech,* 22 (1936): 213–220, 591–602.

Panetta, Edward, "A Rationale for Developing a Nationally Competitive National Debate Tournament Oriented Program." *Argumentation and Advocacy,* 27 (1990): 68–77.

Parson, Donn, ed., *American Forensics in Perspective.* (Annandale: Speech Communication Assoc., 1984).

Perelman, Chaim and Lucie Olbrechts-Tyteca, *The New Rhetoric: A Treatise on Argumentation.* John Wilkinson Purcell Weaver, trans. (South Bend: University of Notre Dame Press, 1969).

Peters, Thomas and Robert Waterman, *In Search of Excellence: Lessons from America's Best Run Companies.* (New York: Harper & Row, 1982).

Pollock, A. "The Relationship of a Background in Scholastic Forensics to Effective Communication in the Legislative Assembly." *Speaker and Gavel,* 19 (1982): 17.

Porter, Sharon B. and Michael Sommerness, "Legal Issues Confronting the Director of Forensics." *National Forensic Journal,* 9 (1991): 109–123.

Ratliff, Gerald L., *Beginning Reader's Theatre: A Primer for Classroom Performance.* (Annandale: Speech Communication Assoc., 1981).

Renz, Mary Ann, "Strategies for Increasing the Use of Ballots in Coaching Individual Events." *National Forensic Journal,* 9 (1991): 167–172.

Roloff, Michael, *Interpersonal Communication: The Social Exchange Approach.* (Beverly Hills: Sage, 1981).

Ross, Raymond, *Small Groups in Organizational Settings.* (Englewood Cliffs: Prentice-Hall, 1969).

Rothenberg, I. F. and J. Berman, "College Debate and Effective Writing." *Teaching Political Science,* 8 (1980): 21–39.

Ruff, H. L., "Teaching Philosophy and Debate." *Speaker and Gavel,* 17 (1980): 162–170.

Scott, Robert L. and Bernard Brock, *Methods of Rhetorical Criticism: A Twentieth-Century Perspective.* (New York: Harper & Row, 1972).

Shimanoff, Susan, *Communication Rules: Theory and Research.* (Beverly Hills: Sage, 1980).

Shurter, Edward D., "State Organization for Contests in Public Speaking." *Quarterly Journal of Speech,* I (1915): 59–64.

Sprague, Jo and Douglas Stewart, *The Speakers Handbook,* 3rd ed. (New York: Harcourt Brace Jovanovich, 1992).

Steil, Lyman K., Larry-Barker, and Kitty Watson, *Effective Listening.* (Reading: Addison-Wesley, 1983).

Stelzner, Herman, "Tournament Debate: Emasculated Rhetoric." *Southern Speech Communication Journal,* 27 (1961): 34–42.

Stepp, Pamela L. and Ralph B. Thompson, "A Survey of Forensics Activity at Selected Colleges and Universities in the United States, 1987." *National Forensic Journal,* 5 (1988): 121–136.

"Timetable for Planning an Invitational Tournament." *Speech Communication Teacher,* (Winter 1989), p. 7.

Thomas, David A. and Jack Hart, eds. *Advanced Debate,* 3rd and 4th eds. (Larchwood: National Textbook, 1987).

Thomas, David A. and Jack Hart, "Ethics in Speech Events: A Replication and Extension." *National Forensic Journal,* 1 (1983): 74–96.

Thomas, David and Stephen Wood, *CEDA: 26th Anniversary Assessment Conference Proceedings.* (Dubuque: Kendall-Hunt, 1993).

Thomas, S., ed. *Studies in Communication: Culture and Communication,* Vol. 3 (Norwood: Ablex, 1987).

Thonssen, Lester and A. C. Baird, *Speech Criticism.* (New York: Ronald Press, 1948).

Toffler, Alvin, *Future Shock.* (New York: Bantam Books, 1971).

Toulmin, Stephen, *The Uses of Argument.* (Cambridge: University Press, 1958).

Trenholm, Sarah, *Persuasion and Social Influence.* (Englewood Cliffs: Prentice-Hall, 1969), Chapter 10.

Ulrich, Walter, "Philosophical Systems as Paradigms for Value Debate." *CEDA Yearbook (1983),* pp. 22–28.

Wallace, Karl W., *History of Speech Education in America.* (New York: Appleton-Century-Crofts, 1954).

Wallace, Karl W., "The Substance of Rhetoric: Good Reasons." *Quarterly Journal of Speech,* 49 (1963): 239–249.

Watzlawick, Paul, Janet Beavin, and Don Jackson, *The Pragmatics of Human Communication.* (New York: W. W. Norton, 1967).

Whately, Richard, *The Elements of Rhetoric,* Douglas Ehninger, ed. (Carbondale: Southern Illinois University Press, 1963).

Willard, Charles, "Argument Fields and Theories of Logical Types." *Journal of the American Forensic Association,* 17 (1981): 129–145. "Special Issue: Review Symposium on Argument Fields." *Journal of the American Forensic Association,* 18 (1982): 191–257.

Wood, Roy V. and Lynn Goodnight, *Strategic Debate,* 4th ed. (Lincolnwood: National Textbook, 1989).

Wood, Stephen C. and Pamela A. Rowland-Morin, "Motivational Tension: Winning vs. Pedagogy in Academic Debate." *National Forensic Journal,* 7 (1989): 81–98.

Index